mama's little
BOOK OF TRICKS

mama's little
BOOK OF TRICKS

› Fun Games › Cool Feats › Nifty Knowledge

by Lynn Brunelle

Illustrations by Jessie Eckel
Technical Illustrations by Arthur Mount

CHRONICLE BOOKS
SAN FRANCISCO

DEDICATION

For Keith, Kai, and Leo, who put me on the mama map.
And for my own sweet mama, Ellen, who still has
a trick or two up her sleeve.

Library of Congress Cataloging-in-Publication Data available.

ISBN-10: 0-8118-5571-6   ISBN-13: 978-0-8118-5571-6

Manufactured in China.
Design by Principle Inc. | www.designbyprinciple.com

Distributed in Canada by Raincoast Books
9050 Shaughnessy Street
Vancouver, British Columbia V6P 6E5

10 9 8 7 6 5 4 3 2

Chronicle Books LLC
680 Second Street
San Francisco, California 94107
www.chroniclebooks.com

LifeSavers Wint-o-Green candy is a registered trademark of The Wrigley Company.
Frisbee is a registered trademark of Mattel Toy Manufacturers.

Acknowledgments

Special thanks to all the mamas who inspire and awe me:
Maura, Debbie, Mia, Cindy, Leslie, Shana, Maryjane,
Ilana, Tracy, Karin, Linda, Lisa, Jay, Jobie, Sylvia, Anne, Val, Laura,
Christine, Carlin, Jennifer, Kris, Annie, Dinah, Rosie, Robin, Erren,
Peggy, Vanessa, Allison, Buffy, Liz, Aunt Jo, Ann-Meg,
Kathryn, Kelly, Cheryl, Sarah, Julie, Sherri, Helen, Deepali,
Jan, Pauline, Susan, Colleen, and Toshi.

And thanks, too, to Kate Renée, Jenna, Bizzy, Alisa,
Pepper, Jodene, Alex, and Amanda—without whose help
I would never have been able to put this together.

→ table of contents

Techno Mama

∗ INTRODUCTION ∗

It happens when you least expect it. Without warning. It happens
to us all. We're driving along; waiting in line (at a restaurant,
in a movie theater, at a doctor's office, in a supermarket, at a
café); on the phone; at home; or just out and about. And
WHAMMO! The kids are bored! They're fidgeting, whining,
winding up, and (uh-oh) starting to melt out of control!

Not to worry! Help is at hand. Just take a deep breath. Slow
down. Have fun. And reach for *Mama's Little Book of Tricks*.
Relive the simple pleasures of life and share them with your kids.
Hang a spoon from your nose, skip a stone, balance the salt
shaker on the table, blow great bubbles, make a whistle out
of a raisin box, and astonish your offspring with stunning facts
about everything from bugs to dinosaurs to body parts.

Page through the following tricks and discover a treasure trove
of stunning gems to entertain the masses. Jam-packed with
tried-and-true secrets, skills, and wow-inducing tricks, *Mama's
Little Book of Tricks* will help you keep your kids amazed,
amused, and entertained—and elevate you to the high
position of coolest mama on the block.

Discover your inner tricky mama. Banish boredom! Delight in
your ability to fascinate, enthrall, and inspire!

You've heard it before, but it's never been more true—
MAMA KNOWS BEST.

TRANSPORTA-
mama

Whether you're behind the wheel of a car,
the wheels of a shopping cart, or up in the air,
here are some of my favorite go-to tricks
for all you go-go mamas.

* cars *

"ARE WE THERE YET?" You've heard it before.
We've *all* heard it ten minutes into a five-hour trip,
the haunting refrain we tormented our own
parents with, coming back to bite us.

> ## backseat games *(Also fun for trains and buses ...)*

Keep a Straight Face

This one's fun for young kids.

1. Everyone agrees on a silly phrase. It can make no sense, like "neener-neener-wah-wah-wah!" or it could be something like "Peter Piper picked a peck of pickled peppers."
2. One player asks any question, such as "What's your favorite color?" or "What did you do this weekend?"
3. The other player has to answer every question with the silly phrase.
4. The trick is not to laugh. Fat chance.
5. Players take turns.

FOR OLDER KIDS

Try taking turns saying anything to make the other person smile.

SMILE!

Everyone smiles and waves to the folks in passing cars and counts how many people smile and wave back. A smile is one point and a wave is two. See who can get the most points.

1. Pick something to count but keep what it is to yourself. (It could be cows, green cars, coffee shops—whatever.)
2. Tell the kids you're going to count something that you see outside the window, but you're not saying what.
3. As you see the item, count the number out loud.
4. The first one to figure out exactly what you are counting gets to be the next secret counter.

→ make up your own wacky songs

Reinvent a few favorite songs. Use the lyrics here or create your own. It's sure to get the kids laughing and dreaming up their own versions.

SUNG TO

"Twinkle, Twinkle, Little Star"

We're all packed in our big car
With snacks and drinks we're going far
Zipping down the twisty road
Mama's got a happy load
Miles and miles in our big car
We have no idea where we are.

"Jingle Bells"

Jingle bells, the backseat smells
Someone spilled their lunch
With cracker crumbs
And chewing gum
So many things to munch!

"Row, Row, Row Your Boat"

Drive, drive, drive the car
Quickly down the street
Wearing a cheeseburger as a beret
And french fries on your feet.

✳ ✳ ✳ ✳ ✳ CLEVER MAMA ✳ ✳ ✳ ✳ ✳

ELEVEN COOL FACTS ABOUT DINOSAURS

1. Fred Flintstone would never have had a dinosaur pet, because people had never existed when dinosaurs lived. People came along about 65 million years after the dinosaurs died off.
2. Most dinosaurs were big, but some were as small as chickens.
3. A velociraptor's claw was about fifteen inches long—as long as a toddler's arm!
4. *Brachiosaurus* was probably the largest dinosaur—about eighty tons and forty to fifty feet tall.
5. *T. rex* was more of a scavenger than a hunter.
6. Most scientists believe birds are descended from dinosaurs. *Archaeopteryx* was the first feathered dinosaur and bird.
7. Alberta, Canada, has a rich dinosaur history. More than thirty-five species of dinosaur fossils have been found there.
8. Dinosaurs flourished for 140 million years, and are the most successful land creatures ever to have lived.
9. If the history of the Earth were compressed into a single year, dinosaurs would appear in August and die out in November. Humans, who have been around for 2 million years, would appear on the last day of December, late in the evening.
10. *Ankylosaurus* was like a tank, with lots of thick, bony armor on its body. It also had a nasty weapon—a heavy club on the end of its tail, which it could swing around and smash into an attacking dinosaur.
11. *Triceratops* had a four-foot-long horn over each eye and one on its nose.

* planes *

What's more challenging than being trapped with small people who don't understand why it's *not* OK to kick the seats in front of them for fun? "And *why* do we have to keep our seat belts on the whole time?" Here are a couple of tricks to keep 'em in their seats.

→ two cool in-flight experiments

Blow the Paper Wad into the Empty Bottle

Here's a challenge that will keep them busy for a while.

1. You need an empty water bottle and a crunched-up paper wad that can rest on the mouth of the bottle and look as if it could easily be blown in

2. Challenge the kids to blow the wad in without putting their lips on the bottle.

3. They'll huff and they'll puff, but they'll never get that wad in.

MAMA'S LITTLE SECRET

▸ ▸ ▸ ▸ ▸ ▸ ▸ ▸

The bottle isn't empty—it's full of air, and when the kids blow, the air inside the bottle pushes the wad out.

Crush a Bottle Without Even Touching It!

The FASTEN SEAT BELT sign has flashed, and the plane is about to begin its descent to your destination. The kids are squirming. It's the perfect time to harness the power of the atmosphere and crush your empty water bottle.

1 You need an empty plastic water bottle.
2 Before the plane descends, open it and then cap the bottle tightly.
3 Place the bottle somewhere the kids can see it.
4 Rub your temples and stare at the bottle as the plane descends.
5 The bottle will be crushed by the time the wheels hit the runway.
6 Stop staring, and shake your head as if coming out of a trance.

MAMA'S LITTLE SECRET
▸ ▸ ▸ ▸ ▸ ▸ ▸ ▸

What's going on is that when you sealed the bottle at the high altitude, the pressure on the inside of the bottle was equal to that outside the bottle. But when you moved from high in the atmosphere, where the outside pressure is not as strong, to the bottom of the atmosphere, where the pressure is very strong, the bottle was crushed.

15

→ the fun bag [What to Pack to Entertain Your Kid in Midair]

Beyond books, baby dolls, and stuffed animals, here are a few find-'em-around-the-house things to pack in a secret fun bag to keep your kids entertained.

Tried-and-true trick-treats to amuse babies under two...

▸ A roll of tape—pulling out, tearing, and sticking tape is hours of fun!
▸ A handful of plastic straws from the beverage cart.
▸ A small stack of paper cups—great for stacking and unstacking. Also fun for putting straws in and emptying them out.
▸ Old magazines—my sons love to tear the pages. Older kids can tear out faces and make collages with the tape right on the tray table.
▸ Sticky-note pad—very fun to deconstruct and stick elsewhere.

For kids two and up, here's what has worked for me over the miles...

▸ A sheet of sandpaper and some lengths of colored yarn—this makes a great portable "drawing" pad. The yarn stays put, and kids can create some fun pictures.
▸ A small metal tray and some magnets—could be alphabet letters, could be tacky magnets you've picked up while on vacation. Doesn't matter. Give the kids a laptop scenario and they may play for hours—OK, minutes!
▸ Index cards and crayons. Fold the cards in half and they stand up. Make a barnyard, train station, hospital, fire station, kitty boutique—whatever they may fancy—and set up a scene on the tray table.

Fun things for kids five and up...

‣ Pack a glue stick, some paper, a pair of scissors, crayons, and markers and let them use in-flight magazines to:
  * Select pictures from magazines, glue them onto paper, and then write a story connecting the images.
  * If you have more than one kid, have them make their collages, then swap and write stories about the other's picture choices.
  * Make face collages. Cut out lips, eyes, noses, ears, and hair and construct a host of faces.
  * Design clothes for paper people. Either cut out clothing, glue it onto paper, and draw people in it, or cut out people and draw clothes around them.
  * Mix it up! Cut out the head of one person, the arms of another, and the legs of another and make a bunch of mixed-up people.
‣ Origami paper and instructions.
‣ A deck of cards for playing games or learning tricks.

✳ ✳ ✳ ✳ ✳ CLEVER MAMA ✳ ✳ ✳ ✳ ✳

FOUR REALLY BAD JOKES

1. What did one hat say to the other hat?
   You stay here. I'll go on a head.
2. Why is ten scared?
   Because seven ate nine!
3. Knock Knock
   Who's there!
   Danielle!
   Danielle who?
   Danielle so loud—I heard you the first time!
4. A woman went to a psychiatrist. "Doc," she said, "I keep having these dreams. First I'm a tepee, then I'm a wigwam, then I'm a tepee, and then I'm a wigwam. It's driving me crazy. What's wrong with me?" The doctor replied, "It's very simple. You're two tents." *Ba-DOOM-bum!*

* bikes *

It's always fun to ride your bike.
There's no secret trick to that, but there are times
when a breeze around the neighborhood feels a little flat.
Liven up the ride with a couple of flashy tricks to get the
bikes looking and sounding new and exciting.

→ how to dress up a bike

With a little colored plastic tape, some crepe paper, a
toothbrush, and paint, you can really deck a bike out for
any occasion.

Go Traditional

1. Wind crepe paper through the spokes, so the flat side
   shows. Use as many colors as you like.
2. Wrap the crepe paper around every surface except the seat.
3. Tape several long strands of yarn, string, or crepe paper
   onto the end of each handlebar.
4. Ride like the wind!

Go Pollock

Introduce your kids to free-spirited modern art.

1. Dip a toothbrush into water-based paint.
2. Scrape across the bristles with your thumb to splatter the bike.
3. Try different colors.
4. Wash it off when you want a change.

Holy Spokes!

1. Get colored plastic straws.
2. Make a cut along one side of a straw.
3. Slip it over a spoke.
4. Repeat for all the spokes on each wheel.
5. Try painting the straws for a different look.

Make Clicky-Card-Spoke Thingies

Remember these? They're still fun. You need a playing card and a clothespin with a spring.

1. Find the rear-wheel fender support, a thin bar that runs past the wheel.
2. Clip the card to it so the card sticks slightly through two spokes.
3. Make sure the card is angled up and back a bit.
4. When the bike moves, the card will flick past the pokes and make a noise as the wheel spins.

✳ shopping-cart ✳ tricks

The idea of shopping with one child, and then two, could strike terror into the bravest of hearts. What do you do when they start to melt down in aisle three? There's always the emergency "open-up-some-package-of-something-who-cares-if-it's-good-for-them-open-it-now!" food. But here are a couple of tricks that let me get a few more aisles under my belt before the sprint to the checkout.

One Fruit, Two Fruit, Red Fruit, Blue Fruit!

This trick works with toddlers, who really want to help out after all!

What You Need:
Shopping cart, food

What You Do:

 Place the child in the large section of the cart.

 Tell him or her that you need his or her help arranging the items that you are going to select.

 Brainstorm how you would like to organize the items. Some ideas that have worked for me:

* Put things into piles of similar color.
* Put things into yummy or yucky piles. Do not worry if one pile is bigger than the other.
* Put things into plant and not-a-plant piles.
* Organize by container—plastic in one corner, metal in another, and paper in another.

4 Hand each item to your assistant, and keep up an ongoing dialogue about the sorting.

5 If you feel like taking it to an extreme, have things bagged in the piles your child has created. *(This makes unpacking groceries fun, too.)*

A-Hunting We Will Go

With older kids who can and want to help, try turning the shopping trip into a scavenger hunt. It takes a little time to prepare—but what's an extra list or two when you're making your own list, right?

What You Need:
A shopping cart, a list for each kid

What You Do:
BEFORE YOU LEAVE HOME
Make a list for each kid—I do this by aisle.
You can do this two ways:

- Straightforwardly   "blueberries," or "five bananas."
- In riddle form, like "I'm small and blue and round and packed in a clear box," or "I'm a long and yellow fruit, and I grow in a bunch."

WHEN YOU GET TO THE STORE

1 Give each kid a list and a section of the cart to call his or her own.

2 Aisle by aisle—so you don't lose sight of them— challenge the kids to complete their lists.

3 Release the hounds.

4 Give treats to the winners.

Go Fish

This trick works with the kid in the kid basket or the big basket. You need a little prep for this trick, but kids are sure to get hooked. Tell your kids you're going fishing and see what they can catch.

What You Need:
A shopping cart, string, a rubber band, small food items

What You Do:
BEFORE YOU LEAVE HOME
1. Cut a four-foot length of string.
2. Tie one end to a rubber band. This is your fishing rod.

WHEN YOU GET TO THE STORE

1 Place the child in the kid basket.

2 Tie the non-rubber-band end of the string to the handlebar of your cart.

Tell your kid this is the fishing pole, and here's the trick:

* He or she has to let out the string and close his or her eyes.
* Then you put something in the rubber band—maybe a banana, an apple, a walnut, a small package of cookies— whatever fits.
* Then tug on the line. Say, "You caught something!"
* With eyes still closed, he or she has to pull up the "catch" and feel it to see what it is.
* Questions are allowed, as is eating the catch once it's been identified. (Just remember to pay for it!)
* Multitask, and select your items as you play. You'll be greeting the sassy checkout gal sooner than you know...

Spell It Out

This aisle by aisle game is fun for older kids who like to puzzle things out. It's a grocery version of I Spy. Pick an item you need, and tell the kids you need something beginning with the letter it begins with—P, for example. They can each bring something back beginning with that letter. If one is right, he or she wins. If not, they bring the item back, and you give them the next letter—I—until one of them finally brings back that pineapple!

MANGIA
mama

Delve into this menu of tricks, whether you're sitting in a restaurant or trying to keep the kids entertained while you rustle up some dinner.

✳ dining out ✳

Kids getting fidgety waiting for the waitperson?
Balance the salt shaker. Hang a spoon from your nose.
Do a couple of straw-assisted impressions.
Or simply master the art of chopstick use. It will keep
them happy until dinner arrives.

Balance the Salt

Defy gravity as you wait for your meal to come.

What You Need:
A salt shaker, salt, a tabletop, strong lungs

What You Do:
1. Challenge your kids to balance the salt shaker on its edge.
2. After they've had a few attempts, grab the shaker with a flourish.
3. Pour a small pile of salt out on the table—enough so you can settle the shaker into the salt on an angle and have the salt support it.
4. After you've done this, gently blow the salt pile away.
5. The shaker stands on its edge, seemingly all by itself (*it's actually still supported by a grain or two of salt*).

Hang a Spoon from Your Nose

This trick is a real crowd pleaser.

What you need:
A metal spoon, a nose,
breath *(preferably fresh)*

What You Do:

1. Do a drum roll on the table for effect, or clink a glass gently with your spoon until all eyes are upon you.

2. Saying nothing, but using expressive eyes, show the spoon to your kids with a flourish. Show them the front and back— as if to say, "Nothing extraordinary about *this* spoon!"

3. Point to your nose for suspense.

4. Take a deep breath, and fog up the inside part of the spoon. You need a lot of breathy fog for this trick to work.

5. Hold the fogged-up spoon to your nose for a few seconds, and then slowly move your hands away.

6. If the spoon flops off, no problem. You can use this as a dramatic element to illustrate how difficult and gravity-defying this trick really is.

7. When the spoon does stick, pause for effect.

The kids will inevitably want to do this themselves. Let them. Hold contests. Who has the most elegant suspension? Who has the most endurance? Time them. When the food finally arrives, the kids will have forgotten how long the wait was.

Impressions with Straws

Need a fast attention-getter? Grab a couple of straws and dive right in. These are two of my favorites, but feel free to improvise and create your own.

What You Need:
Straws, enthusiasm

What You Do:
STRAW WALRUS
This is a classic two-straw move.

1. Remove the paper from two straws.
2. Place one straw over your left upper canine tooth (the pointy one).
3. Place the other over your right upper canine.
4. Position your upper lip over the straws.
5. Clap the backs of your hands together.
6. Say, "A-WHUR a-WHUR a-WHUR," as if you were a barking seal.

STRAW LOBSTER
I call this the straw lobster—or lobstah (I did grow up in Maine, after all). It's really more of a straw termite or earwig, but that's just gross.

1. Take one straw and find the midpoint.
2. Place this part of the straw in your mouth and clamp down firmly.
3. Open and close your mouth to fold the straw and move the "pinchers."
4. Accompany this move with any guttural sound you are comfortable making in a public place.
5. Eye-rolling and brow-furrowing are optional but nice touches.

Master Chopsticks

The "chop" in chopsticks stands for "fast." *(It's a pidgin English version of the Cantonese word **kap**.)* Here's a great trick when you need something fun fast: Practice using chopsticks. Got two sticks? In a pinch, two straws will do. This 3,000-year-old technique is not beyond your grasp!

What You Need:
Chopsticks

What You Do:

1. Hold your eating hand up in front of you, palm out. This will gain attention.
2. Place one chopstick in your hand so it is nestled in the V between your thumb and index finger. Push the stick with your thumb against the inside pad of your middle finger. This stick won't move much.
3. Make the sign for "OK" with your thumb and index finger.
4. Pinch the other chopstick between your index finger and thumb.
5. Move the top chopstick to pinch foods while holding the bottom one steady.
6. To pick up rice, scoop underneath while holding both sticks steady.
7. Once the kids have mastered the technique, toss small objects like sugar packs, ice cubes, or even a lipstick on the table and see who can pick them up chop-chop.

TRICKY CHOPSTICKS TRICK

If your kids are too young to do the master technique, try this trick.

What You Need:
Chopsticks, a paper chopsticks wrapper, a rubber band

What You Do:

1 Fold the chopstick wrapper into a small wad and place it between the sticks about 1 inch from the top.

2 Wrap the rubber band around the sticks and wad twice.

3 Then wrap the sticks above the ball with the rest of the rubber band.

4 Now your kids can use the chopsticks as tongs.

What Are You Having Faux Dinner?

This trick keeps hungry kids captivated until the food arrives. You may need to bring the paper and crayons from home, though some restaurants may have these at the ready.

What You Need:
Paper *(paper tablecloths are great, but any sheet of paper works well)*, crayons

What You Do:

1 Position the paper directly in front of your kids.

2 Ask them what they're having for dinner.

    a. What kind of food?   c. Silverware?   e. Glasses?
    b. Drink?   d. Plates?   f. Napkins?

3 Give them the crayons.

4 Have them draw their place settings, the food, etc. Encourage details!

5 Challenge them to come up with really gross or silly things, like spider-web noodles or real toast "fingers"!

6 They can use the paper as a place mat when dinner comes.

***** CLEVER MAMA *****

VEGGIE OR FRUIT?—FIVE SURPRISES
You may know them as veggies, but they're really fruit.
Technically, anything that bears seeds is considered fruit.

1. Pumpkin   4. Cucumber
2. Eggplant   5. Zucchini
3. Tomato

EAT YOUR FLOWERS!
These "vegetables" are actually flowers.

1. Broccoli   3. Asparagus
2. Cauliflower   4. Artichoke

GROW YOUR OWN PINEAPPLE!
You can grow your own pineapple from a store-bought pineapple.
Just cut off the crown of leaves and plant it in good soil. Place the
pot in a sunny spot and keep it well watered. In about two years,
you'll have fruit!

* dining in *

There's a world of food fun to have while
you wait for fun food!

Tie a Bone in a Knot

After you roast a chicken, save the wishbone and amaze your
kids with this bendy bone trick a few days later.

What You Need:
A wishbone, a jar with a lid, white vinegar, time

What You Do:
1. Without the kids' seeing, soak the bone in a jar of vinegar
   for a week.
2. Rinse it; it should be really bendy.
3. Show the bone to your kids. It won't look any different.
4. Then tell them you will tie the bone in a knot.
5. Concentrate. Make a concentrate-y face.
6. Tremble. Fake a false attempt.
7. Then tie the bone in a knot. The kids will be amazed.
8. Tell them you soaked it in vinegar and it dissolved all the
   calcium, which is what makes your bones hard.
9. Then make them drink milk!

Make an Eggshell Disappear

You have to stretch this trick over three days. The payoff doesn't come till then, but it's fun to build suspense by having the kids check every once in a while.

What You Need:
A raw egg (still in the shell), a jar, white vinegar, time

What You Do:
1. Take the egg and put it in a jar.
2. Cover it with white vinegar.
3. Wait.
4. Watch.

After three days or so, the eggshell will be gone, and what you will have left is a goo-filled membrane. Very gross. Very cool.

**MAMA'S LITTLE
SECRET**

❯❯❯❯❯❯❯❯

Vinegar dissolves calcium, which is what eggshells are mostly made of.

Make Raisins Dance

This one is a popular one in my house. We set it up while I make dinner, and the kids watch the dancing raisins until the food is ready!

What You Need:
A clear drinking glass, water, ½ cup white vinegar,
1 tablespoon baking soda, a handful of raisins

What You Do:
1. Fill the glass half full of water.
2. Add the vinegar.
3. Toss in the baking soda
4. Ooh and ahh over the fizz. (*I have to say that the potion-mixing thing is a fun distraction, and you get this cool fizzy thing happening that wows and amazes, but in a pinch, if you don't have vinegar and baking soda on hand, a glass of clear seltzer will work.*)
5. Toss a handful of raisins in the mixture.
6. Watch. Give it time. Keep watching
7. When the raisins start moving up and down, have the kids provide the music.

MAMA'S LITTLE SECRET
▶ ▶ ▶ ▶ ▶ ▶ ▶ ▶

Raisins are wrinkly. The air bubbles get trapped in the wrinkles and rise to the top, bringing the raisin up. When it gets to the top, the gas escapes and the raisin drops back down.

Tell a Hard-Boiled Egg from a Raw One

When you have a hard-boiled egg, a raw egg, and a bored kid or two or three hanging around, sharpen the kids' powers of observation and experimentation with this trick.

What You Need:
A raw egg, a hard-boiled egg, curious kids

What You Do:
1. Hold up the raw egg and the hard-boiled egg, and ask the kids to figure out which one is which—*without* breaking it.
2. Make a mark on one egg.
3. Offer a few experimentation suggestions:
   a. Float or sink?
   b. Shake and rattle or no?
   c. Stand on end or not?
4. Gather their findings and write them down. How did the marked egg behave? How did the unmarked egg behave?
5. When they finish and come up with their hypothesis, have them each pick their choice of which egg is raw.
6. Now conduct one final eggsperiment! *(I couldn't resist!)* Spin both eggs. The one that spins faster is cooked.

MAMA'S LITTLE SECRET
▶ ▶ ▶ ▶ ▶ ▶ ▶ ▶

Raw eggs are filled with fluid, which sloshes here and there when you spin it. Hard-boiled eggs are solid. so their insides spin in unison with the shell.

Pull Metal Out of Cereal

Iron-fortified cereals are good for you. They provide an important piece of a healthful diet—heavy metal. Want to see? Try this trick.

What You Need:
1 to 2 cups iron-fortified cereal, a resealable plastic baggie, a bowl, water, a fridge magnet (*the bigger and stronger, the better*), a chopstick (*for stirring*)

What You Do:
1. Put the cereal in a few bags and zip them up.
2. Give each kid a bag to crush.
3. Get them to crush the cereal to dust.
4. Empty the cereal dust into a bowl and cover it with water.
5. Toss in the magnet.
6. Stir and stir and stir with the chopstick
   (*for at least five to ten minutes*).

7. Lift out the magnet.
8. Gently rinse it.
9. Look at it.
10. See the tiny, fuzzy iron filings? Small bits of metallic iron have been added to the cereal as a nutritional supplement. Iron-fortified means iron filing–fortified. Don't worry! It's actually good for you!

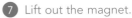

Glow-in-the-Dark Crunch

What You Need:
Wint-O-Green LifeSavers, a dark room, someone to chew, someone to observe

What You Do:
1. Bring the kids to a dark room, and tell them you're going to glow in the dark.
2. Pop a couple of the LifeSavers in your mouth and chew, chew, chew, with your mouth open.
3. Sparks will fly.
4. Let the kids take turns chomping and sparking.

MAMA'S LITTLE SECRET
▸ ▸ ▸ ▸ ▸ ▸ ▸ ▸

When you crunch them, the sugar crystals inside this particular candy break apart and create mini electrical charges that leap and sparkle. The sparks create an ultraviolet light that is absorbed by the wintergreen molecules, which glow. The whole thing is called triboluminescence, if you want to get fancy.

→ april fool's food

Food that looks like something it isn't is a big hit with kids. They love to make these tricky foods and be in on the joke when some unsuspecting adult chomps down and gets a big surprise.

Sushi Cupcakes

These crack me up. They're funny, sassy, and easy to make. The kids like the sophistication of creating "sushi," and these really do look like the real thing. After you make them, try eating them with chopsticks!

What You Need:

A white cake recipe, a mini cupcake tin, white frosting, fruit leather, shredded coconut, chopped-up bits of gummy candy *(red and green and yellow work really well)*

What You Do:

1. Use your favorite white-cake recipe to make mini cupcakes.
2. When they cool, frost them entirely *(including the sides and the bottom)* with white frosting.
3. Cut a length of dark green fruit leather to the same height as the cupcake, and wrap it around the sides *(this is the seaweed)*.
4. Roll the tops and the bottoms in the coconut *(this is the rice)*.
5. Cut the gummy candy into small pieces and insert them in the top to look like tuna, cucumber, or pickled things.
6. Serve on a skinny sushi platter.

Meatloaf Cupcakes with Mashed-Potato Frosting

These look so much like the real deal. They're a hoot to make with the kids, who have a blast eating them and fooling Dad.

What You Need:

Paper cupcake liners, a muffin tin, your favorite meatloaf recipe, mashed potatoes, food coloring (*optional*), eensy-weensy pieces of diced carrot and green, red, or yellow bell pepper (*for sprinkles*)

What You Do:

1. Place liners in the muffin tin.
2. Put the raw meatloaf mixture into the cupcake cups. Fill to the top of each cupcake liner and level it off.
3. Bake at 350° F for about 45 minutes, or until done.
4. Make your mashed potatoes, and really whip them up.
5. You can even tint your frosting by adding food coloring if you like.
6. Frost your "cupcakes" with the mashed potatoes.
7. Add your carrot and pepper sprinkles and serve.

Hamburger Cookies

Fun. Funny. Vegetarian. What's not to like?

What You Need:
Vanilla wafers, thin chocolate-mint cookie, white frosting, yellow food coloring, red food coloring, shredded coconut, green food coloring, a tablespoon of milk, sesame seeds

What You Do:

1. Have the kids help make the components and have them in organized piles.
   a. *The bun: two vanilla wafers*
   b. *The burger: a chocolate-mint cookie*
   c. *The toppings:*
      i. *Cheese: Mix white frosting with yellow food coloring*
      ii. *Ketchup: Mix white frosting with red food coloring*
      iii. *Lettuce: Mix coconut with green food coloring*

2. Assemble the burgers. For each:
   a. *Take a vanilla wafer and turn it rounded-side down.*
   b. *Slather a little "cheese" on it so it drips convincingly over the edge.*
   c. *Place the "burger" on top.*
   d. *Add some "lettuce."*
   e. *Then add some "ketchup."*
   f. *Then put on the other vanilla-wafer bun.*

3. Dip your finger in the milk and get the top of each "bun" moist.

4. Sprinkle on a few sesame seeds.

5. Presto! Burgers!

Put a Lobster to Sleep

You're about to have a glorious lobster dinner, but the kids are worried about the crustaceans feeling pain when you boil them. Not to worry. I learned this trick from a true *lobstah* fisherman in Maine.

What You Need:
A live lobster, patience

What You Do:
Assure the kids that current scientific thinking is that lobsters—being crustaceans—have such a primitive nervous system that they do not have the ability to register pain. *(Evidently pain is bestowed only upon the higher thinkers. Hmm.)* If the kids don't buy into the current scientific thinking, you can hypnotize the lobsters.

1. Grasp the lobster on the back of its body, in front of the tail segments and right behind the joints to the claws.
2. Turn the lobster over. Don't let go. *(I once lost a lobster this way. It fell to the ground and shot itself across the floor, out the door, and into the bushes.)*
3. The lobster may slap its tail repeatedly. It's just going to sleep!
4. Hold the lobster on its back for a minute. It should completely relax.
5. It's now asleep. Do with it what you will.

NATURE
mama

Let's face it, no mama has more tricks up
her sleeve than Mother Nature. Here are a few
inspired by her natural bounty.

Catch a Firefly

Maybe you're camping. Or maybe it's just getting dark out in the backyard, and suddenly there are these moving points of flashing light. Fireflies are fun. There's no trick to them, but there is a cool trick to catching them and making your own lantern.

What You Need:
Fireflies, a clear glass jar, a rubber band, cheesecloth

What You Do:
1. Watch for that first flash and walk over to it.
2. Try and spot the beetle that is hovering in the air before it flashes again.
3. When it flashes, catch it in your cupped hands.
4. Gently drop it into your jar and cover the opening with the cheesecloth.
5. Wrap the rubber band around the cheesecloth at the opening of the jar.
6. Enlist the kids to catch about a dozen fireflies, and see if you can get enough to make a lantern. *(This is what they did in ancient Japan for outdoor lighting!)*
7. Enjoy them for a while, but then let the fireflies out. They're fragile and cannot survive well in an enclosed space.

MAMA'S LITTLE SECRET
▸ ▸ ▸ ▸ ▸ ▸ ▸ ▸ ▸

The light in a firefly's abdomen is created by a chemical reaction inside special cells. If the firefly is moving around and flashing, it's a male. If it's sitting still on a branch or fence, it's a female. Each species of firefly has its own code of flashing. Watch for a pattern in one, and see if you can spot its mate.

NINE COOL BUG FACTS

1. All bugs have six legs. If it doesn't have six legs, it's not an insect. Spiders aren't insects, and neither are scorpions.
2. There are over 4,000 species of bees in America alone.
3. A cockroach can live for nine days without a head.
4. A female praying mantis chomps off the head of her mate before mating. If she didn't, he wouldn't be able to complete the act.
5. Fewer than 1 percent of insects are pests. Most of them pollinate or create silk, honey, and other things the world benefits from.
6. Scientists know of about 1 million species of insects but estimate that there are anywhere from 10 to 30 million species of them on Earth.
7. Butterflies taste with their feet.
8. A flea can jump 130 times its own height.
9. A leaf-cutter ant queen mates only once, just before establishing a new colony. She can then keep the sperm viable for up to fifteen years and produce as many as 300 million offspring.

Mark the Trail

A walk in the woods is fun, of course, but it's every mother's nightmare to lose the kids in the woods. Here's a trick to teach your kids to mark the trail and *not* get lost.

What You Need:
Rocks or sticks

What You Do:

> For a right-hand turn on a trail, place this marker in the path.

> For a left-hand turn, use this marker.

> For straight ahead, use this marker.

> Now turn around as if you were coming back along the trail. Make sure the markers are just as visible from this direction, and see how each marker looks from this perspective.

Three Cool Knots

What could be more fun than slipping the kids a length of rope and telling them to tie one on? Not only are these fun to show, they're fun for kids to practice and they have practical applications, too—like tying up the helium balloon before it soars away, or keeping the old laces tight.

What You Need:
All you need is a piece of string or rope about 2 feet long.

1. SQUARE KNOT

You know this one. It's the one you use to tie shoelaces so they never unlace, or to keep a ribbon tied around a package so you can do whatever you do for a bow. You know it, and your kids might know it, too. It's a nonslip knot—easy to untie if you need to. It's the grandmama of all knots—also known as a Granny knot. Go figure.

Here's how you do it:

1. Take the two ends of a piece of rope. Call the left end "Louie" and the right end "Roger." Cross Roger over Louie to form an X.
2. Take Louie and cross it over and then under Roger, keeping Roger still on the right and Louie on the left.
3. Cross Roger over Louie—now Roger is on the left and Louie is on the right.
4. Loop Roger under Louie, through the loop and over.
5. Pull both ends and tighten the knot.

2. SHEEPSHANK KNOT

Sounds impressive, no? This knot is used to shorten a rope without cutting it. It's a little tricky, but nothing a mama such as yourself can't tackle. Here's how you do it:

1. You don't even have to deal with the ends of the rope for this knot. Make a long Z somewhere in your rope. Each part of the Z should be equal in length—say, six to eight inches.
2. Take the lower right end of the Z and flop it once to make a loop.
3. Now take the top right bend of the Z and tuck it into the loop.
4. Tighten the loop.
5. Repeat this process on the other side and tighten it.
6. Voilà—you have a sheepshank!

3. THE CLOVE HITCH

In the worlds of mulled cider and pomanders, the clove has its own special place, but in the world of knots, the clove hitch is a cool one that allows you to tie onto an object like a loop, post, or maybe even a wayward dog's collar. It can also be used in boating.

Here's how you do it:

1. Start with the object you want to tie on to. Hold both ends of the rope in your hands.
2. Call the left end "Louie" and the right end "Roger."
3. Hang onto Roger and pass Louie around the post.
4. Keeping Roger rather taut, cross Louie over Roger and back around the post again.
5. Tuck Louie in through the loop it makes when going around the pole the second time, and pull both Roger and Louie tight.

Know Your Planets

OK, first things first. What are the planets' names, and in what order do they orbit the sun? Give up? Try this little memory trick:

My Very Exciting Mama Just Swallowed Up Noodles

Weird? Annoying? Maybe, but say it to yourself over and over:

"My Very Exciting Mama Just Swallowed Up Noodles."
"My Very Exciting Mama Just Swallowed Up Noodles."

Then tell your kids. It's a great way to remember the order of the planets. The first letter in each word of this silly sentence starts the name of a planet. Now, things get a little dodgy here, because there are two *Ms:* Mercury and Mars. But in this clever sentence, there is a *Y* in "My"—and one in Mercury as well! *(What will she think of next?)*

So, there's: Mercury, Venus, Earth, Mars, Jupiter, Saturn, Uranus, Neptune. Got it? ...but no more Pluto. Since 2006, it's no longer deemed one of the celestial big guys—now Pluto is considered a dwarf planet.

Know Two Constellations and One Bright Star

While the sky is blanketed with constellations, if you have a couple that you know, along with an ancient story of scandal and mystery, you'll be a backyard-and-campout-mama hit.

URSA MAJOR—THE GREAT BEAR

The Big Dipper is one of the most recognizable constellations in the sky, but technically speaking, it's not a constellation. It's only part of one—part of Ursa Major, or the Great Bear. The handle of the Dipper is the Great Bear's tail, and the Dipper's cup is the Bear's butt. Look up in the sky at pretty much any time of the year and you can probably spot the Big Dipper. Now that you've wowed the kids with your astronomical finesse, use the Big Dipper to find Polaris and the Little Dipper.

POLARIS

Find Polaris, the North Star, by tracing an imaginary line from the bottom right star in the cup of the Big Dipper through the top right star, and then go about five times as far. Polaris is also known as the North Star because it's found almost directly over the North Pole, and all the other stars seem to rotate around it. Its position stays pretty much the same all night.

URSA MINOR—THE LITTLE BEAR

Once you've found Polaris, you'll be smack-dab in the middle of the Little Dipper, which is part of the constellation Ursa Minor, or the Little Bear. Polaris is at the very end of the handle of the Little Dipper. The handle of the Dipper is the Little Bear's tail, and the Dipper's cup is the Bear's flank.

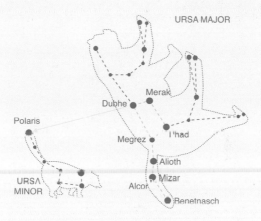

THE ANCIENT GREEK MYTH BEHIND
URSA MAJOR AND URSA MINOR

Zeus, the king of the Greek gods and goddesses, was always getting into trouble with his wife, Hera, because he kept falling in love with other women. One of them was the beautiful Callisto. Hera was furious! So, zap!, she turned Callisto into a bear. Being a bear wasn't easy for Callisto, because she still had human feelings wrapped up in her new big, hairy body. Time passed, and one day she saw her now grown-up son, Arcas, in the woods. She was so thrilled to see him that she ran toward him to give him a huge hug. All Arcas saw was a scary bear barreling down on him, so he drew his bow to shoot. Luckily Zeus, seeing what was about to happen, turned Arcas into a bear, too, so he would immediately recognize his mama. But Zeus's wife, Hera, was still very angry. So to protect them from her fury, Zeus grabbed the two bears by their tails and swung them into the heavens. And there they live together to this day, safely among the stars.

"Hear" Stars Being Born

Looking for a good way to talk about the Big Bang theory of the beginning of the universe? Who isn't? Pick a night when the sky is clear and the stars are twinkling.

What You Need:
The night sky, a TV

What You Do:

1. Look out the window, or go outside and look up at the stars. Be awed.

2. Ask the kids if they want to listen to the stars. Tell them it has nothing to do with Dick Clark. When they ask who that is—well, that's another conversation.

3. Bring the kids into the TV room and turn the television on. Find a channel that has only static. Pause for effect.

4. When they look at you, puzzled, say, "This is what stars being born sound like." Then explain:

   a. *About 13 billion years ago, all the energy in the entire universe was squished into a tiny speck.*

   b. *The speck, as you might expect, exploded with a ginormous BANG, heaving matter (atoms and molecules) outward to make the billions of galaxies of our vast universe.*

   c. *The matter (stuff) and the energy are still out there in the universe. Atoms rearrange, and energy changes form, but it's all the same stuff from the original BOOM!*

   d. *The static on the TV is leftover radiation caused by the Big Bang still zinging around the universe.*

   e. *You can hear it. You can see it. Pretty cool.*

Make a Daisy Chain

Here's a great trick for turning a field of daisies into a fun and engaging project.

What You Need:
Daisies

What You Do:

1. Pick a few dozen daisies, or any other nonpoisonous flower.
2. Cut the stems to about five inches.
3. Use your fingernail to make a small slit through the middle part of the stem.
4. Thread one stem through the hole, and pull it down until the flower is resting against the stem with the hole in it.
5. Make a new hole with your fingernail in the next stem.
6. Take another flower and place the stem through that hole.
7. Continue until you have a chain the length you want.
8. To end the chain and make it into a circle, take the last stem and thread it through the first hole.

Whistle with an Acorn Top

A beautiful autumn day has many beautiful things to share. Chief among the most beautiful are the acorns that drop hither and yon. Their caps make such loud whistles!

What you need:
An acorn top, breath (*preferably fresh*)

What you do:

1. Hold up your acorn top and declare that you will now make a high-pitched whistle.
2. Wait for the kids to be enthralled.
3. Hold the cap in your hands, with the hollow part facing you.
4. Bend your thumbs to make a V at the top of the cap. Your thumbs should cover the rest of the cap.
5. Place your bottom lip on your thumb knuckles and blow down on the V.
6. Wiggle your mouth around until you get the whistle you are hoping for.
7. Blow! Amaze! Breathe. Take a bow!

Whistle with a Blade of Grass

What's cooler than making a wild, whistly noise in the middle of a field?

What You Need:
A nice wide piece of grass that's at least eight inches long, two hands, a deep breath

What You Do:
1. Hold your hands up as if you were praying.
2. Place the grass along the length of and between your thumbs.
3. The blade should be taut from the tips of your thumbs to the heels of your hands.
4. Place your lips on your thumb knuckles (the middle part between them is where all the action takes place).
5. Blow gently on the grass.
6. It should vibrate, and then sing.
7. Start softly, and then when you gain confidence and an audience, you can let out a screamer!

Tell Time by the Sun

This is a fun trick to get the kids to notice time passing and how the sun moves. The clock is easy to make, and the kids get a kick out of checking the sun-clock and marking out the hours. *And it's still fun the next day when you can tell the time with a plate.*

What You Need:
A sunny day, a stick, a paper plate, tape or glue, a watch, a pen

What You Do:
1. Poke a stick through the center of your plate.
2. Anchor it in place with tape or glue *(or both, if you're that kind of mom).*
3. Place the stick-plate in a spot that gets sun all day. Anchor it so it won't move.
4. Check your watch. When it gives you a time on the hour, have the kids locate the shadow on the plate and mark it with the pen.
5. Have the kids make a mark on the plate where the shadow falls every fifteen minutes.
6. The next day, check your clock and try telling the time without using your watch.

Tell the Temperature from a Cricket Chirp

It's hot. The kids are soggy from playing, and they're in need of quick calm-down fun. Listen for crickets. If you hear them, you're in luck. This trick is really interesting.

What You Need:
A chirping cricket, a hot night, a watch, a thermometer

What You Do:
1. Count the number of times one cricket chirps in thirteen seconds.

Add forty and you have a pretty close estimate of the temperature in degrees Fahrenheit.

 Check the number against your thermometer. How close can you get?

Weather Forecasting

Who needs a degree in meteorology when you've got a little weather forecasting help from the Big Mama, Mother Nature?

What You Need:
Any of the following—the evening sky at dusk, frogs, seagulls, a campfire, the moon

What You Do:
1 Memorize the following little nuggets of info, and whip them out whenever appropriate.

2 Make sure to point out to the family every time your forecast is accurate.

> *Red sky at night, sailor's delight.*
> *Red sky in the morning, sailors take warning.*
> You've heard it before, but why does this work? There is actually science behind it all. *(Isn't there always?)* When there are very high clouds in the sky, they scatter the sunlight as the sun sets and rises, turning the light a beautiful red. High clouds mean that a change in weather is in the cards. If you see the cloud color at night, the change could happen and pass by morning. If you see it in the morning, the change could happen during the day.

▶ *With a singing frog comes rain or fog.*
Say you're out hiking in the woods or relaxing in the yard, and you hear the frogs start to kick in croaking. Pack up the picnic and break out the rain boots, because wet weather is on its way. Frogs are happy, happy, happy when their skin is damp. So happily they croak. Damp air precedes rain, so the frogs know about it before we do.

▶ *Snoozing bird? Storm's the word.*
If you ever find yourself passing a field that is full of snoozing seagulls or crows, it's probably safe to say a storm is on the way. Why? Right before a storm blows through, the pressure decreases-and that makes it harder for birds to get up in the air and fly around. so they hang out on the ground until the pressure increases.

▸ *Smoke signals—straight up is clear weather, but a low cloud means rain.*
This is all about pressure. If the pressure is high-a sign of good weather-the smoke from your fire rises straight up. When the pressure drops-a sign of bad weather-lots of itty-bitty dust particles that have been suspended in the air sink down and press the smoke from your fire down..

▸ *Ring around the moon, rain or snow is coming soon.*
Look up at night when there's a full moon. If it's crystal clear, you're in the clear, but if you spot a glowing ring around the moon, here's your chance to shine as a weather forecaster: declare an imminent change in the weather. Why? The glowing ring is actually reflected light passing through a high cloud of ice crystals. High clouds indicate that the weather will change. Depending on the time of year and the temperature, this will probably mean rain or snow.

Measure the Distance from a Storm

Thunder rumbles, lightning strikes—but exactly how far away is the storm? Get the kids to do this trick and it almost makes storms fun.

What You Need:
A storm

What You Do:

1 You see lightning first because light travels faster than sound. So at the first flash of lightning, begin counting—one-Mississippi, two-Mississippi, etc.

2 Stop counting when you hear the thunder.

3 The number you've reached is an estimate of how far in miles the storm is from where you are.

4 It's fun to count while the storm approaches and then as it recedes.

* snow fun *

The next dark and snowy winter day when you hear
the kids say "It's no fun..." Tell them "YES! SNOW FUN!"
and then prove it!

Make a Snow Angel

What You Need:
Snow (*deep enough to flop into*), your body (*preferably
covered in snowproof clothes*)

What You Do:
1. Say, "Did I ever tell you kids what an angel your mother is?"
2. When you have their attention (*after they stop laughing*),
   flop down on your back in the snow.
3. Open and close your legs, and move your arms up over
   your head and back down to your sides, as if you were
   doing a jumping-jack.
4. Repeat five or six times.
5. Gracefully stand up.
6. Regard your masterpiece.
7. Draw a halo on top.
8. Gasp in admiration.
9. Invite the kids to be angelic as well.

For extra fun, try using sticks, pinecones, leaves, acorns, or
even icicles to decorate your angels.

Make a Snowflake Catcher

If the winter weather outside is frightful, run, don't walk outside! With this cool snowflake catcher, the kids will be amazed for hours.

What You Need:
A piece of black velvet *(at least twelve by twelve inches)*, duct tape, a small plate *(plastic is fine)*

What You Do:
1. Place the velvet on a table, fluff-side down.
2. Place the plate upside down on top of the fabric.
3. Use duct tape to secure the velvet around the plate.
4. Flip the whole thing over. The surface should be taut, like a drum.
5. Place the whole thing in the freezer for at least half an hour.
6. Take the snow catcher outside and catch a few flakes. The soft velvet catches the flakes gently and allows enough cold air to circulate around them so they don't just melt.
7. Compare the designs. Use a magnifying glass. Use a flashlight to illuminate them. Count the sides. Ooh and ahh. Fun!

Make a Technicolor Snowman

What You Need:
FOR THE SNOW FOLK:
Good sticky snow, sticks, a carrot, buttons, a hat, a scarf

FOR THE TECHNICOLOR FUN:
Spray bottles, water, food coloring

What You Do:

1 You know the drill—get the kids to make a snowman:

    a. *Roll three big snow boulders—big, medium, and small.*

    b. *Pile the medium one onto the big one, and then the small one on top.*

    c. *Poke two sticks into the sides for arms,*

    d. *Make a face from the carrot (nose) and buttons (eyes).*

    e. *Add a scarf or hat, or any other dress-up items you want.*

2 Now, here's the fun part—add some color

    a. *Fill up a spray bottle with cold water and add fifteen to twenty drops of food coloring, whatever color you want.*

    b. *Shake it up and spray away! Here are some ideas I've tried:*

      i. Make funky clothes:

        A plaid shirt—spray with a wide spray in one color, then change the spray nozzle to stream and spray lines going down, then across for a checkerboard look.

        Perky pants—try playing with patterns and colors to make some loud print pants.

      ii. Skip the buttons and carrots, and experiment by drawing with color. You can make funny mouths and lovely eyes by spraying color.

      iii. Hairdos—sculpt and spray funky coifs.

Make an Igloo

Jack Frost has been dancing around, and the yard is full of snow. Turn an ordinary snowbank into a cool shelter. Just use common sense—if the snow is heavy and dense, it's not a good time to build an igloo for the kids. You don't want it to cave in and hurt them.

What You Need:
A plastic box *(a file storage box is excellent)*, some cooking spray, a shovel, snow, space to build

What You Do:
MAKE YOUR BLOCKS

Spray the inside of a plastic box with cooking spray. Shovel in some good, sticky snow and tamp it down. Tip it over and voilà! You have a snow block.

CREATE YOUR STRUCTURE

1. For an igloo, you'll want a round footprint, big enough for the kids to hang out in—maybe six feet in diameter?
2. Lay your blocks in a circle.
3. Leave space for a door (to be created in Step 11).
4. Have a grown-up inside the igloo and one outside as you layer the blocks up.
5. Each layer of blocks should tip in a bit, so the structure is domed.
6. Fill all the cracks with snow as you go.
7. Continue to work upward, so that the top of the igloo is at about shoulder height of the person working inside.
8. At the very top, there will be a hole that can be filled with one single block.
9. After the igloo is completed, begin to dig downward to enlarge the inner chamber.

10 Cut vents in one or two places for air circulation.

11 Make the entrance using the space you left in Step 3.

    a. Dig a hole in the side from the inside out.

    b. Put two blocks next to the door.

    c. Place a block on top for a roof.

    d. Fill in the cracks with snow.

    e. Dig down to enlarge the opening.

12 Once you're sure your igloo is secure, hop in and make snow furniture, if you like.

13 Before you start to go numb, exit your igloo and enter you nice cozy house for some hot cocoa.

ARTSY
mama

Creativity is really the name of the game.
Whatever the medium—paper, paint, clay, or
performance—celebrate the artist within!

* the play's *
the thing

Kids acting up? Put that talent on center stage!

 → puppets

Almost anything lying around the house can become a new character of its own. A couple of eyeballs and some hair—you'll never look at anything the same way again!

Make a Sock Puppet

You've had it, haven't you? Who hasn't? There is a pile of unpaired socks building up in the laundry room. Stop hoping the matching sock is somewhere to be found. It's gone. It has left you so you can have the fodder for sock-puppet fun.Take advantage of this gift.

What You Need:
A sock, permanent markers, glue, felt, buttons, beads, pipe cleaners, or other decorations

What You Do:
Here's the basic design.

1. Put the sock on your nondrawing hand.
2. Fiddle with it until you get a mouth that works for you by using your thumb and forefinger for bottom and top lips.
3. You can put a stitch in each corner if you want to keep your mouth from moving around, but if you're like me, you won't worry about such things . . .

4 From here, you can decorate the puppet any way you like. Here are some suggestions.

› *Eyes*
  i. Draw with a marker.
  ii. Glue on circles of felt.
  iii. Glue or sew on buttons or beads.
  iv. Use jiggly eyes.
  v. Cut sections of toilet-paper tubes and paint them
  vi. Glue on the spoon parts of plastic spoons and draw pupils on them.
  vii. Use pieces of egg cartons.

› *Ears*
  i. Use triangles of felt.
  ii. Use long U-shaped pieces of felt for floppy ears.
  iii. Glue on pom-poms.

› *Nose*
  i. Glue on a button.
  ii. Draw one with a marker.
  iii. Glue on a pom-pom.

› *Mouth*
  i. Color one in with a marker.
  ii. Glue on a felt tongue.
  iii. Glue on white triangle teeth.

› *Extras*
  i. Glue on pom-poms all over for a polka-dot look.
  ii. Stick pipe cleaners through and bend them to make wiry hairs or antennae.
  iii. Glue on a tuft of fake fur on top, or a line of it for a mane.

5 Voilà! An alter ego worthy of the stage. Make a handful of puppets and create a cast of characters.

Make an Index-Card Puppet

No socks? No problem. You can use any card-stock paper to make a puppet with legs.

What You Need:
An index card or any card stock, scissors, a coin with a diameter as wide as your index finger, markers/crayons, anything you have lying around in your craft pile—feathers, sequins, glitter, pipe cleaners, glue

What You Do:
1. Flip the index card over so there are no lines showing.
2. Put the card on the table so the length is vertical—up and down, not across.
3. Make two circles about ½ inch up from the bottom, using the coin as a template.
4. Cut out the circles.
5. Place your index and middle fingers through the holes. These will be the legs of your puppet.
6. Draw the body and cut it out. Make sure there's at least ½ inch around the leg holes so your puppet doesn't lose its legs.
7. Decorate your puppet with markers, sequins—whatever you like.
8. Stick your fingers in and kick up your heels!

Make an Upside-Down-Chin Face Puppet

Perfect for a rainy day, and good for a crowd. This face transformer is funny just to do and even funnier when the kids start doing shows of their own.

What You Need:
A bandanna, a couch that kids can sit on backward *(with their legs up the back and their heads dangling over the edge),* face paint

What You Do:
1. Loosely tie a bandanna around your kid's face, just below the nose.
2. Have the kid lie down on the couch, feet up the back and head dangling down.
3. Flop the bandanna so it loosely covers the nose and eyes.
4. Use the face paint to paint a nose and eyes on the kid's chin.
5. Add a moustache, eyebrows, even a hairline if you like.
6. Have the kid talk in an exaggerated manner.
7. The other kids will howl. You might want to video this and have the kids create their own plays.

→about face

Masks and face painting can transform any kid—or Mom for that matter!

Tinfoil Masks

Wearing masks only once a year just isn't enough, is it? Whip out the foil and fabricate these fantastic foil-y face masks.

What You Need:
Heavy-duty aluminum foil, scissors, markers

What You Do:

1. Take a twelve-by-twelve-inch sheet of foil and have your kid mold it over his or her face, making sure to get the nose, chin, and eyebrow ridges. You might want to double or triple the foil layers, so it doesn't get completely smashed.

2. Carefully peel the foil off.

3. Cut eyeholes and a mouth hole.

4. Have the kids decorate the masks.

   ➤ *Hair*
      i. Cut fringe in the foil on top.
      ii. Glue yarn to it.
      iii. Make fringy paper and tape it on top.

   ➤ *Facial features: Markers work well on foil, but water-based paints flake off.*

      Freckles, warts, facial hair, tattoos, a clown face, a monster face

Four Cool Face Paintings

It's all about choices. Whether you have one cheek to paint or a roomful of eager blank canvases, it's best to have a few tricks up your face-painting sleeve so the kids feel like they have some choice in the matter. Good to be able to do a flower, a butterfly, and a couple of creepies like snakes and spiders to round out your skills. Here are a few designs I swear by.

What You Need:
Good face paint, good faces

THE BUTTERFLY
Colors: Black, blue, pink, yellow.

What You Do:

1. Use black to outline the butterfly shape on the face.
   a. *I like to start right between the eyebrows and draw two long antennae up the forehead, with curlicues on the ends.*
   b. *Paint a thin cigar shape down the nose—this is the butterfly body.*
   c. *Do the wings—draw up over the brow, up on the forehead, then around the eyes coming in at about eye level, before swooping out and down over the cheek.*
   d. *Make the bottom of each wing about parallel with the lower lip, and come in to the side of the nose about halfway up.*
   e. *Try to be symmetrical.*
2. Add blue.
   a. *Cover the eyebrows in long strokes that move away from the eyes.*
   b. *Make long strokes under the eyes.*
3. Add pink.
   a. *Starting from where you left off, blend a little pink in with the end of the strokes and continue the outward sunburst effect.*
4. Finish the wings with yellow.

THE SNAKE

Boys love this one. Go figure. Start small on a cheek, or start on the forehead and snake the whole face!
Colors: Black, green, red, blue, yellow.

What You Do:

1. Offer a choice of colors.
2. Outline the snake in black:
   - a. Draw a backward S with an extra squiggle.
   - b. Make the head-end and the tail-end pointy.
   - c. Want stripes? Draw stripe outlines—you'll fill them with color later.
3. Fill in the head. I like to make the heads black, but green, red, and blue can look good too.
4. Draw the eyes on the side of the head.
5. Make a snake's forked tongue
6. Draw circles around the tail if you want rattles.
7. Fill in your spots or stripes.

THE SPIDER

Great for Halloween. Perfect on a cheek.
Colors: Black, green, red.

What You Do:

1. Paint a black circle for the body.
2. Paint a smaller black circle for the head.
3. Paint two green spots for eyes. *(If you want to be technical, draw eight eyes—spiders have multiple eyes! Ick! And cool!)*
4. Paint a red dot inside each eye.
5. Paint eight legs that come off the body.
6. Extra: If you want a black widow, paint a small red hourglass on the belly.

FLOWER POWER
Small flowers on the cheeks are real crowd pleasers.
Colors: Green, yellow, red, blue, orange.

What You Do:
Experiment on paper first to get a look you like.
Here are some ideas:

1 Start with the center of the flower.
- *Try making several small dots of, say, green or yellow for the center*
- *Or try making one larger circle in yellow or green.*

2 Make the petals:
- *Long, skinny red petals*
- *Heart-shaped blue petals*
- *Teardrop-shaped orange petals*
- *Wavy purple lines*

3 Make the leaves with green—make them the same shape as the petals.

4 Make the stem:
- *Try a straight stem coming down the cheek.*
- *Make a wavy vine that winds around the flower and disappears behind the ear.*

mama tip: Be confident: Really load up your brush with color, and use long, confident strokes. No one wants a nervous Nellie painting quick, panicky lines. If you make a mistake, wipe it off and start again.

Use One Piece of Paper to Make Three Costumes for a Play (You *Must* Pay the Rent!)

Use a piece of paper or even a napkin to costume a trio of characters for a dramatic story.

What You Need:
A piece of paper or a napkin

What You Do:
MAKE THE WARDROBE:

1 Fold the paper in half the long way.
2 From the bottom, fold up one inch and crease.
3 Flip the paper over and fold it again.
4 Repeat this process to make an accordion fold.
5 Pinch it in the middle and fan out the edges.

PERFORM THE PLAY:

1 You hold in your hand the hair bow for the Woman in Distress, the mustache for the Villain, and the bow tie for the Hero. When each character speaks, hold the costume in the appropriate place.
2 For each character, use an appropriate voice.
3 Perform the following skit as quickly and as cornily as you possibly can:

You *must* pay the rent!

(Villain—hold the paper as a mustache)

I can't pay the rent!

(Woman—hold the paper as a bow in your hair)

You *must* pay the rent!

(Villain—hold the paper as a mustache)

I *can't* pay the rent!

(Woman—hold the paper as a bow in your hair)

You *must* pay the rent!

(Villain—hold the paper as a mustache)

I'll *pay* the rent!

(Hero—hold the paper as a bow tie)

My hero!

(Woman—hold the paper as a bow in your hair)

Curses! Foiled again!

(Villain—hold the paper as a mustache)

***** **CLEVER MAMA** *****

TEN GROSS HUMAN-BODY FACTS

1. During your lifetime, you will urinate over 12,000 gallons—enough to fill a pool!
2. You are covered head-to-toe with bacteria—believe it or not, they protect you from disease.
3. Your body is more than 60 percent water.
4. You sweat at least a pint a day.
5. Your small intestine is over twenty feet long!
6. When your stomach is empty, it's volume is about a pint. When you're stuffed, it stretches to hold about eight pints!
7. You have no muscles in your fingers.
8. Your skull is made up of twenty-two bones that are bound together with fibers so they won't move.
9. Babies are bonier than grown-ups. They have about 300 bones, which will eventually fuse into about 200 by adulthood.
10. Hair is dead. It is made up of keratin—material left behind by dead cells.

Four Shadow Animals

It's dark. Maybe the kids can't sleep. Maybe you're camping, and you need something to do. You have a trusty flashlight and a wall. With a little finger origami, you can make an ostrich, a bunny, a dog, and a flying bird, and create a show!

The Technique:

1. Turn the flashlight on.
2. Prop it up on something so it stays put. You want the light to be pretty far away from the wall—five to six feet.
3. Stand with your hips parallel to the light's beam.
4. Experiment with where your hands make the best shadow. Close to the light and far from the wall is probably best.

The Animals:
OSTRICH

1. Put your right arm straight out in front of you, palm down.
2. Touch your index finger to your thumb in a pincer-like movement. Your other fingers may extend up in a dainty gesture. This is your ostrich mouth.
3. Bend your arm at the elbow to create the long neck.
4. To make the eye, bend your middle finger and place the tip next to the knuckle of your index finger.
5. Straighten the ring finger so that the tips of the index finger, ring finger, and pinkie are all in a line above the thumb.
6. Move your thumb in a jaunty manner to create a sassy speaking ostrich. Add animation by bobbing the long neck.
7. Rapid wrist twists are also good for ostrich-like behavior.
8. A high-pitched opera voice is suitable for an ostrich.

BUNNY

1. Stretch your right arm out directly in front of you, palm up.
2. Bend the palm toward you so the fingers are straight up.
3. Make a peace sign. These are the bunny's ears.
4. Tuck your thumb under your ring finger and pinkie.
5. Turn your wrist so the bunny faces away.
6. Hop. Hop. Hop.

DOG

1. Extend your arms in front of you. Bring your hands together palm-to-palm, thumbs up.
2. Spread your thumbs a bit to make a V for the ears. Waggling the ears can make for a pretty expressive dog.
3. To make the brow, lift your left index finger straight up and bend it over your right hand.
4. Wiggle your pinkies together up and down. This is the dog's mouth.
5. Woof deeply.

FLYING BIRD

1. Extend your arms directly in front of you palms up.
2. Cross your right wrist over the left one.
3. Link your thumbs.
4. Flap and flutter your fingers for wings.

★★★★★ CLEVER MAMA ★★★★★

CROCODILE OR ALLIGATOR?

Crikey! You can be the mom kids are in awe of when you can tell the difference between these reptiles at the drop of a hat.
The big differences:

1. Shape of the jaw:
    Crocodiles have longer and more pointy V-shaped snouts.
    Alligators have shorter, U-shaped jaws and snouts.
2. Teeth
    Because their jaws are narrower, you can see both the upper and lower sets of crocodile teeth. Think "Croc-o-dile, crooked teeth."
    Alligators have little pockets in their upper jaws where the lower teeth fit in perfectly, so you don't see their bottom teeth when they're just hanging out.
3. Color
    Crocodiles are light tan– or olive-colored.
    Alligators are black.
4. Habitat
    Crocodiles are found most often in salt water.
    Alligators prefer freshwater.

* paper, paint, *
crayon & clay

Need I say more?

→ paper

I find myself saving bits of paper—from cereal boxes to newspapers to coffee filters—just to play with the kids.

Seven Fun Things to Do with a Newspaper

1. Roll up open pages into long tight tubes, and tape them with masking tape. Use these to build structures like houses, tepees, cubes, etc.

2. Roll up tight tubes of newspapers, and tape them together to make furniture.

3. Open a sheet of newspaper, and fold three inches over, and then crease and fold over three more inches until you get a long flat tube. Make ten tubes and weave them together to make a sitting mat.

4. Roll sheets of paper into balls and tape them into shape. Juggle them. (See page 102.)

5. Roll sheets of paper into tubes. Tape them together and roll marbles through them. Create long marble courses.

6. Unfold several sheets of newspaper and place them—open—on your kid's head. Roll the edges and tape them to create a hat. Then decorate as you like.

7. Make an old-fashioned newspaper hat:
    a. *Take a full size piece of newspaper and fold it in half, top to bottom.*

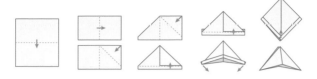

b. Fold it again from side to side, crease it, and unfold it.

c. Fold the top left corner to the middle crease and make another crease.

d. Repeat with the other side.

e. Fold the bottom flap upward. Flip the hat over, and fold that side's flap up as well.

f. Tuck the corners into the hat.

g. Open it up and sport your fabulous headwear!

✳ ✳ ✳ ✳ ✳ CLEVER MAMA ✳ ✳ ✳ ✳ ✳

EIGHT COOL MUMMY FACTS

1. Ancient Egyptians believed that you needed your body in the afterlife. So those that could afford it had their dead bodies preserved by mummification.
2. When a king or queen or royal person died, his or her servants, pets, and family would often be killed, mummified, and buried along with him or her as company in the afterlife.
3. The first step to mummification was removal of the brain through the nose.
4. King Tut was eight when he became king and married his sister, and was eighteen when he died. Some say he was murdered.
5. It took seventy days to make a mummy.
6. Anubis, the god of mummification, has a human body and a black jackal's head.
7. The organs of an Egyptian mummy were kept in jars and buried with the body.
8. Between the layers of wrapping, the ancient Egyptians placed amulets (charms) to protect the body during its journey through the underworld.

Six Fun Things to Do with Paper Cups

1 Turn them upside down, paint them, and glue them onto an old garbage can to make a monster puppet.

2 Line them up in a triangle shape and toss pennies into them. Mark them with point values, and have the kids see how many points they can get. Or write a fortune at the bottom of each cup and have kids toss until they get a fortune.

3 Put a little sand in the bottom of one cup, and securely tape another cup mouth-to-mouth over it. *(Duct or packing tape works well.)* Make several of these, and line them up like bowling pins. Use a tennis ball to knock them over.

4 Paint them as small houses or buildings and create a village.

5 Put a small handful of uncooked rice or beans in the bottom of one cup and securely tape another cup mouth-to-mouth over it. Shake! Shake! Shake! You have a maraca!

6 Make a rain stick:

　　a. *Take 6 paper cups.*

　　b. *Place a handful of uncooked rice in one and set it aside.*

　　c. *Now securely tape two cups together bottom-to-bottom. Use a sharp pencil to poke about 6–8 holes through both bottoms. Make sure the holes are big enough for rice to fall through.*

　　d. *Now securely tape a cup mouth-to-mouth to each open end.*

　　e. *Tape a cup to one end, bottom-to-bottom.*

　　f. *Poke holes through both bottoms.*

　　g. *Turn the stack of cups upside down so the open end of the cup is on the bottom.*

　　h. *Tape this mouth-to-mouth to the cup full of rice.*

　　i. *Flip your stack and enjoy the soothing sounds of rain!*

I'm not going to lie and say this is easy. Origami isn't easy, and every single "Easy Origami" book you see out there simply isn't. But origami is really fun and really engaging, and making mistakes and weird folds and getting a little frustrated is half the fun. Especially when you end up with a darn-cute little frog or penguin at the end.

PENGUIN

What You Need:
A black piece of paper cut into a perfect square.
(If you have origami paper, it will already be cut perfectly.)

What You Do:

1 Fold sides in half diagonally so they meet in the center.

 2 Fold back bottom half of lower triangle.

3 Fold inner tips of flaps under. *Hint: Fold toward front, crease, then fold under.*

 4 Fold top flap down *(about halfway)*, crease, and unfold.

5 Make shorter fold with tip.

 6 Fold tip up.

7 Fold top portion down along existing crease *(created from step 5)*.

8 Fold piece in half vertically toward back.

1 2 **9** Hold the piece at 1, and pull piece 2 up, and then flatten.

10 Fold bottom-right section inside. Repeat on opposite side. Fold tip down slightly.

FROG

What You Need:

A piece of paper—the stiffer the paper, the higher the frog can jump.

What You Do:

 1 Make the paper square by taking the bottom right corner and folding it up along the left hand side of the paper.

2 Then cut the excess paper rectangle off and unfold the paper.

 3 Fold the top and bottom edges together and unfold. Then fold the right and left edges together and unfold.

4 Fold each corner into the center point.

 5 With a point at the top and bottom, fold the right and left sides in and line the edges up along the center line and make a crease. It should look like an upside-down kite.

Take the small triangle at the bottom and fold it up to form a triangle.

 Take the two bottom corners and fold them so they touch the middle line.

0 Fold the bottom part up along the dotted line to form a rectangle.

 Then fold the top half of this rectangle down. These are your frog's legs.

 Now fold the point part down to create a head for your frog and decorate as you will.

11 Admire your amphibian.

12 Make it hop by pressing gently on the back (see the spot marked "X") until the butt touches the legs and let go quickly.

13 Experiment with hopping techniques and have a race.

Make Awesome Paper Snowflakes

The secret to making a great paper snowflake is in the folding. All snowflakes—no matter how different they look—have six sides. This folding technique allows the paper snowflake to have six sides as well, making it an accurate jumping-off point for a scientific discussion of the crystalline properties of snow. Plus, it just makes a pretty paper flake.

What You Need:
8½-by-11 inch white paper, scissors

What You Do:

1. Fold a paper square in half diagonally to form a triangle. The larger the square, the easier it will be to cut.
2. Fold the triangle in half.
3. This is the tricky part—you're going to fold this triangle into thirds. Fold the top third of the triangle partway down, as shown.
4. Fold the bottom third up over the first and flatten the creases.
5. Flip this over and cut a straight line across, as shown. If you cut a curved line here, you get a different look—experiment and have fun.
6. If your kids are freestyle cutters, let them go, but if they like a bit more structure, get them to draw their designs first and then cut, cut, cut!
7. Unfold the masterpiece and express delight! One fun thing we've done is make a bunch of snowflakes and hang them from threads taped to the ceiling to create a "snowstorm."

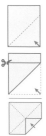

Make a Paper Fortune Teller

What You Need:
A square piece of paper, a pen

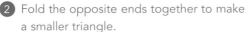

What You Do:

1. Fold the piece of paper from corner to corner to make a triangle.
2. Fold the opposite ends together to make a smaller triangle.
3. Unfold the paper completely.
4. Fold one corner to the centerline.

5. Fold the opposite corner to the centerline.

6. Fold the remaining points to the centerline to get a square.

7. Unfold and pull the four ends together, making a diamond-like shape. Pick up each of the four square flaps, and put your fingers inside. You will be able to move the four parts around.

8. Write four different colors on the outer flaps.

9. Write the numbers 1-8 on the inside flaps.

10. Lift the numbers and write eight fortunes on the under flaps. Pick any you like. Some ideas:

The answer to your question is YES!

Help your mother with chores!

Today is your lucky day.

Be careful today.

Eat five servings of fruits and vegetables a day.

Make a Kite ▶

Go fly a kite. Really! Make one from scratch, and have a little fun with design and aerodynamics while you're at it.

What You Need:

A sheet of 8½-by-11-inch paper *(pretty colors are fun)*, ½-inch-wide masking tape, one eight-inch wooden or bamboo skewer, a plastic bag cut in a one-inch-wide spiral all around *(about six feet makes a great tail)*, a hole punch, string, a stick on which to wind the string

What You Do:

1. Fold the paper in half to 8½ by 5½ inches. *(I grew up calling this a hamburger fold, because it results in a short, squat piece of paper, as opposed to the hot-dog fold, which results in a long, skinny piece.)*

2 Place the fold on your left. Take the lower left-hand corner and bring it to about one inch up from the bottom right. Fold along that diagonal.

3 Open to the fold and tape it firmly to form the kite shape. This fold and the tape will act as the spin of the kite.

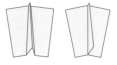

4 Place a skewer flat on the kite, from the upper left-hand corner to the upper right-hand corner, and tape it firmly in place. There's your kite!

5 Tape one end of your plastic ribbon-tail to the bottom-center fold.

6 Flip your kite over and make sure the front flap stands straight up.

7 Punch a hole through the flap, about one-third of the way down. I like to place a small piece of tape over the hole and punch the hole out again to make it strong.

8 Thread your string through the hole and tie it in a knot.

9 Tie the other end of the string in a knot around the stick, and wind the string up on the stick.

10 Go fly your kite.

→ paint

Good to have. Good to make.

Make Finger Paints ▶

Messy, yes. But easy to clean up, and oh-so-fun to play with.
Whip up a batch of homemade finger paints for your pint-size
Picasso.

What You Need:
3 tablespoons sugar, ½ cup cornstarch, 2 cups water, ¼ cup
dishwashing soap, 2 drops vanilla extract, paper cups or small
jars with lids, food coloring (or tempera paint)

What You Do:

1. Combine the sugar and corn-starch in a saucepan.
2. Slowly add the water.
3. Cook over medium heat for five minutes, stirring constantly, until you get a clear goopy mixture.
4. Take it off the heat and let it cool.
5. Add the liquid dishwashing soap and stir to smooth.
6. Add the vanilla extract (for a nice smell).
7. Divide into cups and stir in food coloring or tempera paint.

Make a Rainbow of Colors from Only Three Paints

You're out of green, and the kids are dying to paint a meadow scene. Or, tragically, they want to paint Barney, and there's no purple. What do you do? A little magic mama color mixing can restore a full palette.

If you have your primary colors—yellow, red, and blue—as well as black and white, there are really no colors you can't make:

Blue and yellow make **green**.

Red and blue make **purple**.

White added will lighten any color.

Black added will darken any color.

Red and yellow make **orange**.

White and red make **pink**.

Green and red make **brown**.

Orange and blue make **brown**.

Purple and yellow make **brown**.

Draw a Face

Drawing a face for your kids is a fun way to pass some time, but giving kids the basics to looking at and drawing faces is even cooler.

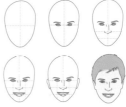

What You Need:
A pen/pencil/crayon, paper

What You Do:

1. Look at faces.
   Really look at them—in magazines, in crowds, or in the mirror
   - *Where are the eyes, really? You want to draw them at the top of the face, but look—they're really in the middle of the face, about halfway between the chin and the top of the head!*
   - *The nose? It goes from the eyes halfway to the chin.*
   - *How big are the ears? The tops are in line with the eyebrows, and the bottoms are level with the bottom of the nose.*
   - *How big is the mouth? Pretty big, really—it's as wide as an imaginary line from one pupil to the other.*

2. Map the face:
   a. *Draw an oval.*
   b. *Divide the face in half from side to side.*
   c. *Divide the face in half from top to bottom.*
   d. *Divide the bottom half of the face into thirds.*

3. Draw a face:
   a. *Draw the eyes so the midline goes right through the center of them.*
   b. *Make the nose so it ends just below the next line down.*
   c. *The mouth should sit right on the next line down and stretch the distance from one pupil to the other.*
   d. *The ears should start just above the eyes and end just below the nose.*

4. Now look around. Study people's faces, and experiment by drawing different kinds of features.

→ crayon stuff

Who doesn't love the smell and feel of a crayon doing its thing on the paper? Try these new ways of using an old favorite.

Recycle your Crayons

Nevermore can your kids claim the crayons are used up, because here's a fun way to take all the old bits and make something new and cool.

What You Need:
Crayon bits, a muffin tin, aluminum foil, cooking spray, an oven

What You Do:
1. Break up all your crayon bits into small pieces, and make piles of like colors.
2. Line the muffin cups with foil and spray the foil lightly with cooking spray.
3. Fill the cups with any color combination that thrills.
4. Put the whole shooting match in a 300° F/150° C/mark 2 gas oven and let it melt. It could take ten to twenty minutes.
5. Take out the muffin tin and let it cool completely.
6. Pop out the new crayon-cakes, admire them, and color your world!

Faux Stained-Glass Window

This is just the trick for brightening a gloomy day.

What You Need:
Waxed paper, a crayon sharpener, crayons, newspaper, an iron, a permanent marker *(optional)*

What You Do:
1. Have the kids draw something. Tell them it is illuminating—or will be!

2. Trace the drawing on a piece of waxed paper.
3. Make sure to draw outlines around the major color areas.
4. Use a crayon sharpener and crayons to make piles of shavings for the colors you want.
5. Sprinkle the shavings in the appropriate areas.
6. Cover the whole piece with another piece of waxed paper.
7. Put a piece of newspaper over it.
8. Iron it on a low setting for thirty seconds to a minute, until the wax melts together.
9. Let it cool.
10. Cut out the original drawing shape.
11. Redraw the black outline with the marker, if you like.
12. Place it in a window and enjoy the illumination.

Design a Pillowcase

Did you know that you can use crayons to make permanent artwork on fabric? Maybe you already know this. Maybe you need to move the perspective a tad to think "artwork," not "stain." I learned the hard way, but as I always say, "Use your mistakes!" Kids can't sleep? Need a project to do in the wee hours? This trick can be dreamy.

What You Need:
A cotton pillowcase, crayons, cardboard, an old towel or some newsprint-type paper (with no ink, or it will come off on the drawing), an iron

What You Do:
1. Get the kids thinking about dreams. What do they like to dream about?
2. Whip out a pillowcase and some crayons.
3. Put a piece of cardboard inside the pillowcase.
4. Have the kids draw their dreams.

Cover the whole thing with an old towel or some newsprint.

 Iron it on a low setting for at least a minute or so. Check to see if the wax has melted into the fabric. When it has, lift the towel or paper off.

 Voilà! Put it on a pillow, toss it at your kid, and tell him or her to sleep on it!

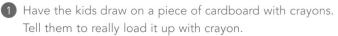

mama tip: This can also work for one-of-a-kind tablecloths when cousins are over for holidays. They can draw to their hearts' content—add messages, and you can make it permanent for the holiday dinner. It really jazzes up the kids' table!

Nuke-It Art

Trying to make dinner, but the kids aren't thrilled about the same old crayon-and-paper routine? Here's a trick: Zap it. That's right, use a microwave to heat things up and you can create a really cool effect in no time at all.

What You Need:
Cardboard, crayons, a microwave oven, a microwaveable cup of water

What You Do:

1 Have the kids draw on a piece of cardboard with crayons. Tell them to really load it up with crayon.

2 Stick the drawing in the microwave. Put a cup of water in for safety's sake so the masterpiece doesn't end up in flames.

3 Now zap it for thirty seconds. Watch it the whole time, and turn off the oven when the crayon has melted.

4 Let it cool. You get this cool, melty look that looks a little like oil paint.

5 When it's cool, you can add more crayon color and zap it again.

→ make your own play clay

Easy as pie—or pie dough, at least! Make a batch of this no-cook, simple dough and keep it in a covered container for at least two weeks of molding, mashing, and mucking around.

What You Need:
2½ cups flour, ½ cup salt, 1 tablespoon alum,
3 tablespoons oil, food coloring

What You Do:
1. Mix the flour, salt, and alum together in a bowl.
2. Add the oil and mix until you get a good dough consistency.
3. Add a few drops of food coloring to the whole batch to make one color, or separate the dough into different bowls and make a rainbow of colors.
4. Keep the clay in an airtight container when you're not using it.

MAMA'S LITTLE SECRET
❯❯❯❯❯❯❯❯

> **The alum keeps bacteria growth in check.**

SPORTY
mama

A stone that skips effortlessly
across the water…A cartwheel executed to
perfection (kind of)…Just do it!

Skip a Stone

A lake, a pond, or even the smooth ocean is a great invitation to skip stones. Here's a technique that will make a splash or two.

What You Need:
Flat smooth stones, a body of water

What You Do:
1. Hold the stone flat-side down. Your index finger should wrap around the back, pointing forward, and your thumb should be on top.
2. Stand sideways with your throwing arm away from the water.
3. Bend your knees slightly and crouch.
4. Using a sidearm toss, throw the stone down and out, and flick your wrist at the end.
5. Throw the stone fast and low so it hits the surface of the water almost parallel and skips along.
6. The stone should roll off your index finger and spin in the air.

→ two frisbee throws and one fancy catch

OK, how cool is Mama when she plays Frisbee in the first place? Now wow them with two (count 'em) ways to throw the disc. Wear a bandanna if you must, and make sure to flash the "hang loose" hand sign every once in a while.

Backhand

What You Do:

1. Grip the edge of the disc with your right hand (*reverse these directions if you're a lefty*), so that all your fingers are wrapped around the edge of the disc from top to bottom and your thumb lies along the top.
2. Step forward with your right leg.
3. Extend your throwing arm across your body, and swing your arm away from your body, releasing the disc when your arm is about forty-five degrees from your body with a snap of the wrist.
4. Keep the disc level as you throw!
5. The power behind your throw should come mostly from the snap of your wrist and partly from the movement of your arm.

Forehand

This is a cool toss, but it takes practice. Practice *alone*, not in front of the kids. It's not cool when Mama throws the disc into the ground and then watches it roll into a pond.

What You Do:

1. Use the first two fingers and thumb of your right hand to grip the disc.

    a. *Place your middle finger on the rim of the underside of the disc.*

    b. *Extend your index finger toward the center of the disc on the underside.*

    c. *Rest your thumb on the top of the disc, wrapping it around the edge.*

2. Stand with the disc to your right, horizontal to the ground. Hold it even with your body, maybe slightly behind you.

3. Step forward with your right foot—yes, your right. Trust me—it seems odd, but it works.

4. Move the disc back and snap your wrist forward, moving your arm forward slightly also.

5. Let go when your arm and wrist movement bring the disc in front of you.

6. Your first few throws will likely hit the ground hard and roll a long way. Fix this by tilting the outside edge of the disc toward the ground before you throw.

7. When you're ready, showcase your disc talents at the next picnic or beach event. Act like it's no big deal. Then teach the kids.

One Fancy Catch

If you're good at catching a Frisbee one-handed, sass it up a little by lifting up your right leg and catching the disc behind you as it speeds under your leg. Practice. When you have it mastered, flaunt it.

→ make two paper airplanes

OK, so one's an airplane and the other is a kind of helicopter thingy. But they're both pretty easy to make, and they're really great fliers.

AIRPLANE

1. Fold a sheet of 8½ x 11 regular printer paper in half lengthwise. Unfold it so that the crease is "valley"-side up.
2. Fold the top corners down to the center fold, making a triangle.
3. Fold the tip down and crease along the bottom of the triangle.
4. Fold about one inch of the tip up; unfold.
5. Fold the top corners down to the center fold at an angle so that the corners meet above the fold in the tip. (Note that the top—the nose of the plane—should be blunt.)
6. Fold the tip up.
7. Fold the entire plane in half so that the tip is on the outside.
8. Fold the wings down. Trim and fly!

Once you've made all of your folds and the plane looks symmetrical, it's time to trim it, or adjust it, for flight. Give it a gentle toss forward. Your goal is to have it glide smoothly and gently to the ground, either flying straight or in a gradual curve. Make these adjustments, if necessary:

- If the nose drops and the plane dives into the ground, bend up the back of the wings. A little bend goes a long way.
- If the nose rises first and then drops, the plane is stalling.
- Bend down the back of the wing. Keep your adjustments small.

When you get the plane to balance on the air and float down gently, then you can give it faster tosses.

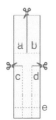

THE HELICOPTER
What You Need:
A piece of paper about four inches by one inch.

What You Do:
Copy the diagram onto the paper and then cut along all the solid lines.

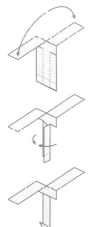

1. Fold flap A forward and flap B to the back.
2. Fold flaps C and D both forward along the dotted lines.
3. Fold along the line E upward and fold tabs around the back to give it weight at the bottom.

Just drop the helicopter with the blades facing upward and the weight at the bottom facing downward for a twirly flight.

⁎ coordination ⁎

Spin a Ball on Your Finger

Maybe you can't slam-dunk the ball, but with this trick, your kids will be in awe. It takes a bit of practice, but when you have it down—watch out, Globetrotters! Mama's in da house!

What You Need:
A basketball

What You Do:

 Find a spot with a lot of room and privacy to practice.

 Get the spin down:

    a. *Stand up with your weight balanced evenly on each leg. Hold the ball about a foot and a half in front of your face, with your arms bent at a ninety-degree angle, and one hand on either side of the ball.*

    b. *Throw the ball up with a quick snap of the wrists while rotating your hands. Cross one arm over the other and follow through, with your fingers pointing in opposite directions.*

    c. *Spin the ball a few times in the air with your hands, and let it drop. Speed is the key to spinning, so keep this exercise up to get the fastest possible speed.*

③ Balance the ball:

    a. *This time, when you spin the ball, don't let it drop. Instead, put your index finger under the axis of the spinning ball. Let the force of the spin do the work.*

    b. *Be patient—keep with it.*

 Dazzle the kids.

Catch a Coin off Your Elbow

What You Need:
A coin, an elbow

What You Do:
1. Do this outside, preferably where flying coins won't break things.
2. Stand with your feet shoulder-width apart, and place your right thumb up against your ear, with your elbow pointing straight out.
3. Place a coin on the flat part of your arm, right above the elbow.
4. Take a deep breath.
5. Open your hand and snap your elbow down toward your hip, catching the coin in midair.
6. Used to catching one? Try adding coins in a stack. How many can you do? How many can the kids do?

Do a Somersault

Remember these? They're still fun to do on sunny days, on the lawn or on very plush carpets.

What You Do:
1. Squat like a frog, and put your hands on the floor in front of your feet—knees out or in, whichever you prefer.
2. Tuck your head, and place the top of your head on the floor.
3. Push with your feet until your butt goes flying over your head.
4. Roll until you land on your feet again.
5. Stand up, arms over your head.
6. Make a crowd noise.

Do a Cartwheel

OK, I was never good at these in my prime, but I can cobble through one. Here's the thing—do one and then teach the kids. They'll go wheeling all over the yard, and that's what you want anyway, right?

What You Do:

1. The trick, really, is the rhythm of the skill—which is "1, 2, 3, 4," or "hand, hand, foot, foot"—as well as getting through being upside-down for any amount of time, however brief. Stand in a lunge position, with your right leg in front. Bend your knees slightly, and raise your arms up on either side of your head.
2. I like to punctuate my cartwheels with a "Hi-*yah!*" If that works for you, here's the place.
3. Reach forward with your right arm, and place the right hand on the ground, kicking your left leg up as you do so.
4. Your left hand isn't far behind, hitting the ground as your legs fly in the air. As it touches the ground, your right leg should be off of the ground also.
5. There is a brief moment when both feet are off the ground and you are supporting yourself in a handstand. It's brief but noble.
6. Your left leg will then reach the ground, followed by the right.
7. Finish in the lunge position, but with the opposite leg in front.

Juggle

What Mama isn't adept at juggling? Why not hone the skill and garner a few giggles while you're at it?

What You Need:

Three oranges (*they may get bruised, so prepare to use them for juice!*)

What You Do:

1 Start by tossing one orange in a nice arc from one hand to the other. The high point of the arc should be a few inches above your forehead. The plane of the arc should be about a foot in front of your face. Practice until the toss is smooth and the catch is effortless.

2 Now try two oranges—one in each hand. Toss the left one into the air—same arc. When the orange gets to the middle point, toss the right one to the left—same arc as with the first one. Catch the oranges. Practice this way until you can make two smooth effortless tosses and catches.

3 Drum roll—now three. Start with two oranges in your right hand and one in your left. Toss one orange from your right hand in an arc to your left hand. When it hits the mid-point, toss the orange in your left hand to the right. When it hits the midpoint, toss the remaining orange from your right hand to your left.

4 By now, you should sense the rhythm that you need to keep this going. Don't freak out if all you do is drop the oranges. Keep practicing. Soon you'll be ready for Barnum & Bailey!

PLAYFUL
mama

In which is revealed the mysteries of the ages—
card tricks, physical impossibilities, how to make
a balloon animal ... Plus a few inappropriate
tricks guaranteed to offend and amuse.

Wiggle Your Nostrils

It's easy to do. Flare and unflare your nostrils as fast as you can. It takes practice to flare and unflare the old nostrils without changing your expression. But when done correctly, this can be a great silent and secret message of affection between you and your kids when necessary.

Crack Your Nose

This one is fun when there's a lull in the action. It evokes horror and delight—and even more delight when the kids learn it themselves and practice it on Dad, friends, and Grandma.

What You Need:
Your hands, your nose

What You Do:
1. Set the scene: Wiggle your nose. Look as if you might sneeze. Say, "Ugh! I need to crack my nose!'
2. Wait for the kids to watch
3. Place your hands together over your mouth and nose with your fingertips, just below your eyes on the bridge of your nose.
4. Secretly place both thumbs in front of your front two teeth, with the thumbnails facing your teeth.
5. Wiggle your hands, and adjust them as if you're getting ready to do something that might be painful.
6. Take a deep breath.
7. Close your eyes.
8. As you bend your nose sharply to the side, snap your thumbnails past your teeth.
9. Use your drama skills. React to the crunching. Open your eyes wide and say, "Now *that* was good. Now I can breathe!"
10. Turn to the closest kids and ask if they want theirs done.

Four Impossible Kid Challenges

. . . and why they can't do them. Got a few smarty-pantses hanging around? Try these challenges.

› The Challenge:
Bet you can't pick up a dollar bill on the floor in front of you.

The Setup:
1. Have the kids stand with their heels against the wall, feet together.
2. Place a dollar bill in front of each kid.
3. Tell them they can have it if they can bend over and pick it up without moving their feet or bending their knees or falling down.

The Trick: Your money is safe. It's impossible to do this because the center of the kids' gravity is over their feet. When they bend, the center moves forward—so if they can't move their feet, they'll topple.

› The Challenge:
Bet you can't blow up a balloon in a bottle.

The Setup:
1. Get an empty two-liter plastic soda bottle and a balloon.
2. Push the balloon into the bottle, and wrap the opening of the balloon around the opening of the bottle.
3. Challenge the kids to blow up the balloon.

The Trick: Even the biggest blowhards won't be able to blow up the balloon. Since there's already air inside the bottle, someone would have to compress and crush that air in order to blow up the balloon. Human lungs aren't that strong.

› The Challenge.

Bet you can't tear a piece of paper into three pieces.

The Setup:

1. Fold a regular 8½-by-11-inch sheet of paper into thirds.
2. Open it up.
3. Cut the creases up to about ½ inch from the top.
4. Have the kids hold both ends, and challenge them to rip the paper so that the middle piece just drops down.

The Trick: Paper tears at its weakest point. Though the two cuts may look equal, there's really no way to do that, so one side will always tear before the other.

› The Challenge:

Bet you can't keep your fists together.

The Setup:

1. Ask a kid to hold both fists together, one on top of the other.
2. Tell the kid he or she will never be able to keep the fists together. *Never!*
3. The kid will try.
4. When he or she is ready, point both index fingers and hold them about a foot apart, with the kid's fists in between.
5. Quickly sweep your fingers past each other—one pushing the top fist and the other finger pushing the bottom fist in opposite directions.
6. They'll pop apart with little effort every time.

The Trick: The kid will put all his or her effort into pushing the two fists together—so a sideways force will easily push the fists apart. Here's a tricky trick. Have the kid try to do the same to you—but don't let him or her see you're holding your bottom thumb in your top fist. They'll never break apart. Tricky Mama!

* making music *

Blow, bang and squeeze to beat the band—
or to make the band.

Whistle with an Empty Raisin Box

One mama's trash is another's treasure. Don't throw out that
empty raisin box; use it to start a band.

What You Need:
An empty raisin box

What You Do:
1. Tear off the box-lid flap and the two tiny side flaps.
2. Place the entire opening in your mouth and seal your
   lips around it.
3. Blow gently until you get a harmonica-like sound. Increase
   or decrease the airflow to create sounds.

Make a Kazoo

Even if the only musical instrument you can play is the radio,
this homemade kazoo will have you and your kids humming in
no time at all.

What You Need:
A piece of paper, a comb, scissors *(optional)*

What You Do:
1. Tear or cut your paper so it is as long as your comb and
   twice the width.
2. Fold the paper in half.

3 Place the back of the comb into the crease.

4 Loosely hold the paper and the comb together.

5 Place the papered comb up to your lips and hum through your mouth *(make an "oooh" kind of sound)* into it.

Juice-Glass Xylophone

Got a fidgety audience whining for dinner—and it's twenty minutes away? This is a real countertop crowd pleaser in our family.

What You Need:
Eight glasses *(or glass bottles)*, chopsticks *(a pencil will work, too)*, a pitcher of water, food coloring

What You Do:

1. Declare a musical interlude.
2. Place the glasses on the counter in front of the kids. (*I put a dish towel down first, because this can get pretty drippy.*)
3. Give each kid a chopstick, and get them to *gently* tap a glass to hear the sound.
4. As they tap, fill the glass and ask them to notice the difference. (*FYI, the more water, the higher the pitch.*)
5. Challenge the kids to create a scale. When they finish, they can try and make a song—"Twinkle, Twinkle Little Star" is always a safe try.
6. They can color the water for added amusement.

Perform an Armpit Fart

Though this is commonly considered a daddy trick, it is possible for a mama to eke out a small sound—but it takes practice. You might want to start in the summer, in a bathing suit. It actually works well when you are wet. When you become more adept, you can continue the fun by sliding your hand to your underarm underneath your winter wear.

What You Need:
Your hand, your armpit

What You Do:
I'm right-handed and, it turns out, right-pitted. I can only do this with my left hand and my right pit. Follow the directions if you're right-pitted, and reverse them if you're a lefty.

1. Cup your left hand.
2. Hunch your back slightly, and lift your right elbow up and out to create a small pocket in your armpit.
3. Place your cupped left hand neatly over the pocket, put your thumb on the front of your shoulder.
4. There should be an air bubble inside your hand/pit.
5. Squeeze abruptly and swiftly by cranking your right elbow down toward your side and squeezing the air out of the pocket.
6. You should hear a sound. If you don't, experiment with your hand placement.

→ six total tongue twisters

Feeling punchy after a long day together? Why not exploit the situation and go for some belly laughs with these tongue-tangling twisters?

- Bad blood, good blood.
- Six thick thistle sticks.
- Toy boat. Toy boat. Toy boat.
- One smart fellow, he felt smart.
- Unique New York
- The myth of Miss Muffet.

→ balloon animals

Who needs to hire a birthday clown—
be one! Here are two simple balloon
animals: a duck and a dog.

DOG
What You Need:
A long balloon

What You Do:
1 Stretch the balloon out
and back until it's a little relaxed,
and then blow it up halfway.
Tie a knot in the end.

2 Make the face:
   a. *Start at the end with the knot and twist a bubble about
   four fingers long. Twist it three times and hang on to it,
   or it will unwind.*
   b. *While holding onto the twisted balloon, make another
   bubble of the same size. This will be the one of the ears.*
   c. *Make another same-size bubble. It should look like this:*

   d. *Bend the balloon so that joints A and B come together.
   Twist them around each other three times. These are the ears.*
   e. *Make another bubble about two to three fingers long and
   twist; hang onto both parts. This is the neck.*

3. Make the body:

a. *Make the front legs:*

   i. Make a two-to-three-finger-
size bubble. Don't let go!

   ii. Make another one of the
same size.

   iii. Just as in Step 2d, bend the
first bubble back to the second one and twist them
around each other three
times.

b. *For the body, make a four-finger-
size bubble and twist.*

c. *Make the back legs:*

   i. Make two more two-to-three-
finger-size bubbles.

   ii. Twist them back on each
other for the back legs.

d. *There should be a small bubble
left over—this is the tail.*

DUCK

What You Need:

An eleven-inch round yellow balloon, two long orange balloons

What You Do:

1 Make the body, by blowing up the eleven-inch round balloon
three-quarters of the way.

2 Make the bill:

a. *Blow up a long, skinny orange balloon two-thirds of the way
and tie a knot*

b. *Make a bubble about three to four inches long and twist
three times.*

c. Take the knot end of the long balloon and wrap it around the first joint to make a loop. Wrap the knot end around and then through.

d. Make the next bubble about five inches long and twist.

e. **Hold onto the balloon,** or it will untwist, and make another three-to-four inch bubble.

f. Take the end of the balloon and wrap it around the second joint to make another loop on the other side.

3 Make the face:

a. Take the round yellow balloon with the knot facing down and twist the top third into a bubble. Twist three times. The small part is the head, and the big part is the body.

b. You will need to hold on to both parts; otherwise it will untwist.

c. Carefully wrap the orange balloon around the yellow one at the joint, and twist the two joints of the orange balloon together three times.

4 Make the feet:

a. Take the other long orange balloon and blow it up two-thirds of the way. Tie a knot.

b. Tie the ends of the balloon together and fold the balloon in half.

c. Twist the opposite sides together. This will create the feet.

d. Take the feet at the twisted joint –and wrap the nozzle from the duck's body into the feet at the knot in the feet.

→ two card tricks

These are true tricks, and you can play them in one of two ways. You can be the trick doer and amaze the kids and remain a cool Mystery Mama, or you can trick them first, then show them so they can trick others. You decide. Either way is pretty fun.

JUMPING JACK

What You Need:

A deck of cards, salt

What You Do:

1 Before you appear in front of the kids:
   a. *Find the jack of hearts and remove it from the deck.*
   b. *Shuffle the deck.*
   c. *Cut the deck.*
   d. *Place the jack at the bottom of the top half.*
   e. *Sprinkle some salt on the top of the bottom stack and place the two halves together.*

2 In front of the kids:
   a. *Ask the kids if they've heard of jumping jacks. Tell them you're about to show them the real Jumping Jack.*
   b. *Place the deck on the floor with a flourish.*
   c. *Get a kid to come and gently nudge the deck with his or her toe to divide it into two piles.*
   d. *Pick up the top pile and show the kids.*
   e. *That's right, JACK!*

COME TO MAMA
What You Need:
A deck of cards

What You Do:

1 Before you appear in front of the kids:

    a. *Place the queen of clubs and the jack of spades on top of the deck.*

    b. *Then place the queen of spades and the jack of clubs right under them.*

2 In front of the kids:

    a. *Tell the kids that when Mama calls, **everyone** listens— even royalty.*

    b. *Pick up the top two cards—the queen of clubs and the jack of spades—and quickly show them to the kids. Do **not** name the cards! (This is the trick—the kids will remember the black-suit queen and jack.)*

    c. *Take the two cards and place them somewhere in the deck.*

    d. *Now tap the deck and say, "Come to Mama!"*

    e. *Get a kid to come up and take the top two cards and show them to the others. Though the spades and clubs have been switched, that detail is pretty small, and it's subtle enough to get 'em every time.*

→ two coin tricks

Got any change? Here are two coin tricks that will occupy and amaze.

FIND THE PENNY (or Nickel, Dime, or Quarter)

What You Need:
A handful of pennies *(or coin of your choice—all the same kind)*, a hat *(or a bag)*

What You Do:

1. Toss the coins into the hat.
2. Have one kid select a coin and examine it without showing you.
3. Make sure he or she notes the date and the mint mark.
4. Have him or her pass it to the next kid, who should also examine it. Continue until all the kids have seen it.
5. Have the last kid drop the coin back in.
6. Shake the hat and immediately grope around with a concentrated face.
7. Select the warmest coin.
8. Pull it out and amaze the kids.

THERE'S A HOLE IN THAT TABLE
(Dear Liza, Dear Liza!)

What You Need:
A tabletop, a coin, a paper cup, a paper towel

What You Do:
1. Sit down at a table, and make sure the kids are on the other side.
2. Tell them you can make a cup go through the table.
3. Knock on the table surface. Ask the kids if it's solid.
4. Place the coin on the table.
5. Place the cup over the coin.
6. Cover the cup with the paper towel, and loosely form the towel into the shape of the cup.
7. Lift up the cup and focus on the coin. Place your finger on the coin and rub it on the table in small circles and hum for effect.
8. Make sure the kids are focusing on the coin.
9. Drop the cup in your lap still holding the paper towel.
10. Place the towel (in the shape of the cup) over the coin
11. Pretend to smash the cup down into the table.
12. At the same time, let the cup fall to the floor from your lap.
13. Look amazed.
14. Lift the paper towel. The coin is still there!
15. Smile knowingly and mysteriously.

→ three key yo-yo tricks

Get the kids a yo-yo—but before they even wind it up, make sure you can do a power throw, do a little sleeper action, and walk the dog to make sure they know who's the MAMA!

THE POWER THROW

This is the first thing you need to know. Practice alone, so you can be flawless in front of the kids.

1 Make sure the string is tied loosely around the axle of the yoyo.

2 Wind it up.

3 Put the string loop around your ring finger.

4 Hold the yo-yo in your hand and curl your arm up as if you were flexing your muscle, with your hand next to your ear.

5 Bring your elbow down with a snap as you release the yo-yo out over the ends of your fingers.

6 The yo-yo should arc out and down. As soon as it reaches the bottom of the string, turn your hand over, and the yo-yo will climb the string and return to your hand.

THE SLEEPER

It's called this because it sits, spinning on the end of the string, allowing you to wow and amaze with tricks galore!

1. Hold the yo-yo correctly in your hand and curl your arm up as if you were making a muscle, with your hand next to your ear.
2. Bring your elbow down with a snap as you release the yo-yo out over the ends of your fingers.
3. The yo-yo should stay spinning at the end of the string. Before it slows down too much, turn your hand over (*palm down*) and give it a slight upward jerk to bring the yo-yo back to your hand.

WALK THE DOG

Now that you can "throw a sleeper," it's time to walk the dog.

1. Throw a fast spinner.
2. Gently lower the yo-yo until it barely touches the floor.
3. The yo-yo will start moving forward on the floor. It's the doggie walking! Whistle and walk along with it.
4. Be sure to jerk the yo-yo back to your hand before it runs out of spin, or you will be performing another trick—the sleeping dog.

→ eight jump-rope songs

1 A my name is Alice
And my husband's name is Arthur,
We come from Alabama,
Where we sell artichokes.
B my name is Barney
And my wife's name is Bridget,
We come from Brooklyn,
Where we sell bicycles.
C my name is ....
And my husband's name is ....
We come from ....
Where we sell ....
(Continue throughout the alphabet)

2 A, B, C, and vegetable goop.
What will I find in my alphabet soup?
A, B, C, D, E, F, G…
*(When you miss, make up something that starts with
the letter you missed on.)*

3 Bubble gum, bubble gum, chew and blow,
Bubble gum, bubble gum, scrape your toe,
Bubble gum, bubble gum, tastes so sweet,
Get that bubble gum off your feet!
I asked my parents for fifteen cents
To see the platypus jump the fence.
She jumped so high she touched the sky,
And didn't come back till the Fourth of July.

4 Miss Lucy had a baby
And she named him Tiny Tim.
She put him in the bathtub
To see if he could swim.
He drank up all the water.
He ate up all the soap.
He tried to eat the bathtub
But it wouldn't go down his throat.
Miss Lucy called the doctor,
Miss Lucy called the nurse.
Miss Lucy called the lady with the alligator purse.

5 Teddy bear, teddy bear,
Turn around.
Teddy bear, teddy bear,
Touch the ground.
Teddy bear, teddy bear,
Show your shoe.
Teddy bear, teddy bear,
That will do.
Teddy bear, teddy bear,
Go upstairs.
Teddy bear, teddy bear,
Say your prayers.
Teddy bear, teddy bear,
Turn out the light.
Teddy bear, teddy bear,
Say good night.

Miss Mary Mack, Mack, Mack
All dressed in black, black, black
With silver buttons, buttons, buttons
All down her back, back, back.
She asked her mother, mother, mother,
For fifteen cents, cents, cents,
To see the elephant, elephant, elephant,
Jump the fence, fence, fence.
He jumped so high, high, high.
He reached the sky, sky, sky,
And he never came back, back, back
Till the Fourth of July, lie, lie.

7 Cinderella, dressed in yellow
Went downstairs to kiss her fellow.
How many kisses did she give?
One, two, three, four, five...

8 Early in the morning, about eight o'clock,
What should I hear but the postman's knock?
Up jumps *(say someone's name)* to open the door,
How many letters did she find on the floor?
A, B, C, D...

* rocks & sticks *

Four Fun Games You Can Play
with Rocks and Two to Play with Sticks

Horror of horrors! You've arrived at the beach, the park, the picnic, or wherever—and you forgot the action figures, the dolls, and the toy cars. You can still capture the kids' imaginations and get them having fun with a couple of treasures like rocks and sticks.

→ games with rocks

Pebble Prowl

One thing that works for me if we're at the beach and the kids need a little direction is to set up a treasure hunt.

What You Need:
A pebbly beach

What You Do:

1 Select a kind of rock, such as:

> *All white and smaller than a golf ball*
> *Dark and smooth*
> *Ones with a stripe*
> *Speckled*
> *Heart-shaped*
> *Looks like a face*

2 Have the kids find as many pebbles fitting the description as they can within a certain time period.

3. A fun variation is to make a list of different kinds of rocks they all need to find, and set up a time limit and award a prize for the kid who gets the most items on the list.

4. Create a display of the found treasure. You can even bring the collections home and keep on collecting wherever you find rocks.

Rock Toss

Here's a good trick to have up your sleeve when the kids are on the beach complaining that there's nothing to do. If you don't have a ton of people around you *(you certainly don't want to wallop anyone with a pebble)*, this is fun, and it will keep the kids entertained for a while.

What You Need:
A few players, pebbles, a sandy beach

What You Do:
1. Each kid selects a pebble that is different enough from the others to use as a marker—for instance, one kid might have an all-white pebble, another an all-black one, etc.

2. Make the game court by drawing a circle in the sand, about twenty-four inches in diameter.

3. Inside that circle, draw a smaller circle—about twelve to eighteen inches in diameter.

4. Inside that circle, draw an even smaller circle about six inches in diameter.

5. About ten paces away, draw a line.

6. Let the kids take turns tossing their pebble into the circle.

7. They can keep score:
   a. *The outer circle is worth one point.*
   b. *The next circle is worth five points.*
   c. *The small circle is worth ten points.*

8. The kid with the most points after ten tosses *(or whatever)* wins.

Who Has the Pebble?

What You Need:
A few players, a pebble

What You Do:

1. Gather the kids in a circle.
2. Choose someone to be "It."
3. "It" closes his or her eyes while everyone else passes the pebble around the circle.
4. Someone holds on to the pebble, and everyone pretends to hide it behind their backs.
5. "It" opens his or her eyes and has to guess who has the pebble.
6. "It" gets three guesses to find the pebble. A correct guess means "It" exchanges places with whoever had the pebble. No correct guess in three tries means he or she is "It" again.

Mancala

This is an ancient African game that takes a little bit of effort to get up and running, but the payoff is grand. Nowadays, you can find it in stores as a board game, but originally it was played with pebbles and little pits dug into the ground. The fun of this is threefold: collecting rocks, making the board, and then playing. If the kids like it, keep the pebbles in a bag and take them with you whenever you'll be outside and kids can dig pits to make the game board. Mancala is great for picnics or camping. *(You can also make a great travel version out of a cardboard egg carton, pebbles, and two plastic cups.)*

What You Need:
A patch of dirt or sand where you can dig little pits, thirty-six pebbles

What You Do:

 Make the game board:

    a. Dig twelve little pits—two rows of six, just like an egg carton.

    b. On either end, dig two larger pits.

When you're done, it should look like this:

2 Set up the game:

    a. Players sit opposite each other, with the board in between.

      ❥ The row closest to each player is his or her row.

      ❥ The big pit on the right is his or her pot.

    b. Place three pebbles in every single pit (but not in the big pots)

    c. Choose who goes first.

3 Play the game:

    a. The first player takes the pebbles from one of the pits on his or her side of the board and, moving counterclockwise, drops one pebble in each pit until the pebbles run out. If the player reaches one of the big pots, he or she drops a pebble in if the pot's on the right (because that's the one that belongs to the player), but skips over it if the pot's on the left (because that's the one that belongs to the opponent).

    b. If the player's last pebble on that turn goes into the player's big pot, he or she can go again.

    c. The game ends when one player clears all the pits on his or her side of the board.

→ games with sticks

Knock It Down

What You Need:

One large target stick at least two feet tall, a small throwing stick for each player—each about one foot long and one inch in diameter

What You Do:

1. Plant the tip of the target stick in loose ground or sand. It should be wobbly enough that it can be knocked down by a flying stick.

2. Measure off anywhere from six to ten paces, and make a line on the ground. This is where the kids will throw from.

3. Kids take turns tossing their stick at the target stick. *Hint—they should use the same kind of sidearm throwing motion used when skipping stones (see page 95).*

4. The first player to knock over the target stick wins.

5. Extend the game by making the first person to knock the target over five times the winner.

Slicky Foot Relay

What You Need:

At least four kids, a one-foot-long sturdy stick for each pair of kids

What You Do:

1. Divide kids into teams of two.
2. Place each stick about twenty-five feet away from each team.
3. At the start, one kid from each team runs to the stick and, without using his or her hands, gets the stick between his or her feet and hops back to the start, tagging the next kid in line.
4. The next kid picks up the stick between both feet, hops back to the original spot, and then runs back, tagging the next in line.
5. Continue until all players have had a chance to go. The winning team is the one that crosses the finish line first.

* three tabletop * games

Sidelined for some reason and can't go outside
to play? Be a hero and set up the kitchen table for
some big-game action.

Tabletop Football

What You Need:
A sheet of 8½-by-11-inch paper, a table

What You Do:
MAKE THE FOOTBALL

 Fold the paper lengthwise *(I grew up calling this the hot-dog fold)*. Crease the paper.

2 Fold this in half lengthwise again to get a column.

3 Now, starting from the bottom, as if you were folding a flag, fold the right bottom corner up about one inch to the left side, making sure the sides are flush, to make a small triangle.

4 Take the bottom point on the left and fold it up, making the sides even to keep the triangle shape.

5 Keep folding the triangle up and over until you get to the top.

6 Tuck the extra flap into the opening so it won't unfold. Make the sides even.

TO PLAY THE GAME

 Get the kids to clear the table. (*Aha! Can you see the beauty in this?*)

2 You need two players to sit at opposite ends of the table.

 Flip a coin to see who goes first.

4. The player who goes first positions the football flat in front of him or her and flicks it with a finger to the other side of the table. Wherever it lands is where the next player starts. (If it goes off the table, it's put back up on the table, halfway between the end and the center line.

5. The receiving player then has four flicks—or downs—to try and get a touchdown. A touchdown is scored when the football is on the table but some part of it—even just a fraction of it—hangs over the edge.

6. The player who scores a touchdown can decide to kick for an extra point.

    a. The other player holds his or her fists on the table, index-fingertips touching together and thumbs up to create the goalpost.

    b. The scoring player positions the ball anywhere behind the halfway line by placing the tip of the ball on the table and the pointy side toward the goal.

    c. He or she then flicks the ball and tries to get it through the goalposts.

7. A touchdown is worth six points, and an extra point is worth one point.

8. If a player doesn't get a touchdown after four flicks, the ball is in the position of the defending player who now gets four flicks to try and score.

9. You can play for a set time and see who has the most points at the end—or play until the first player reaches, say, fifty points.

Tabletop Hockey

This fast winter sport can be played inside all year, and you don't even need any ice.

What You Need:
Craft sticks, electrician's tape, a large yogurt container, lightly sticky masking tape, a milk or juice-container lid

What You Do:
MAKE THE HOCKEY STICKS
1. Cut off one-third of a craft stick.
2. Tape it at a right angle to a whole stick.
3. Wrap the whole thing with electrician's tape.

MAKE THE GOAL NETS
1. Cut off the top half of a yogurt container.
2. Cut that in half to get two semicircular curves for two goal "nets."
3. Use the masking tape to tape the goal nets in place at each end of the table.

TO PLAY THE GAME
Using the lid as a puck, each player uses his or her stick to score goals in the other's net. You can play for a set time and see who has the most points at the end—or play until the first player reaches, say, ten points.

Tabletop Golf
This rain-or-shine golf course is easy to make and can be as challenging as the course architects want to make it.

What You Need:
Paper, scissors, colored markers, tape, coins *(all the same kind, as many as you have players; these will be the "balls")*

What You Do:
MAKE THE COURSE
1. Your tabletop is your course. Decide how many and where the "holes" will be and design them.
2. Draw each green and cut it out.

3. Create and cut out hazards, such as water, sand pits, even aggressive ducks.

4. Draw a "hole" the size of your coin on each green.

5. Secure the greens down on the table with tape.

TO PLAY THE GAME

1. Each player takes a coin and marks it with a different color.

2. Players take turns teeing off and tossing their coin to the hole.

3. As in a real game of golf, the player furthest from the hole goes first.

4. Your score is the number of throws it takes for your coin to hit the hole. *(Any part of the coin hitting any part of the hole is in.)*

5. If your coin hits a hazard, add one stroke.

6. If you toss off the table, add another stroke.

＊＊＊＊＊ CLEVER MAMA ＊＊＊＊＊

EIGHT TRICKY RIDDLES

1. What gets wetter and wetter the more it dries? *A towel.*
2. What runs but can't walk and is in front of you every step of the way? *A nose.*
3. What can you catch but not throw? *A cold.*
4. What goes around the world but stays in the corner? *A stamp!*
5. What is weightless but something you can see? And if you put it in a bucket, it will make the bucket lighter? *A hole.*
6. What is as light as a feather, but can't be held even by the strongest person in the world for much longer than a minute? *Breath.*
7. Where does yesterday follow today and tomorrow? *In the dictionary.*
8. If you drop a yellow hat in the Red Sea, what does it become? *Wet!*

TECHNO
mama

I speak not of your techno-beat (*although a cool mama always knows a few smooth dance moves*), but of your inner geek. These tricks are a blast (*one of them literally*).

Make a Pop-Bottle Rocket

This one's a real blast, but you'll want to take it outside. Make sure you're in an open space where no one can get beaned by a propelled cork.

What You Need:
1 cup white vinegar, an empty plastic two-liter soda bottle, a paper towel, 2 tablespoons baking soda, a cork that fits the bottle snugly

What You Do:
1. Pour the vinegar into the empty bottle.
2. Open the paper towel and place it on a flat surface.
3. Put the baking soda in the middle of the paper towel.
4. Roll the paper towel into a tight tube narrow enough to get through the mouth of the bottle.
5. Twist the ends so you have a baking soda pellet.
6. Get the cork ready, and shove the baking-soda pellet into the bottle and cork it very quickly.
7. Give the bottle a little swirl and stand back.
8. It takes a few moments for the vinegar to get to the baking soda and react.
9. Blast off!

Make Your Own Bubble Goo

You'll never run out of bubble fun if you have a few handy-dandy bubble-making ingredients around.

What You Need:
½ cup dishwashing liquid, a container with a lid *(yogurt containers work well)*, 4½ cups water, 4 tablespoons glycerin *(you can get this stuff at the drugstore or at craft stores)*, a pipe cleaner

What You Do:

1. Pour the dishwashing liquid into the container.
2. Add the water and the glycerin.
3. Put on the lid and give the whole thing a shake.
4. Open it up and let it settle.
5. Bend your pipe cleaner into a loop and twist it shut.
6. Dip the loop and blow.

Make Slime

This stuff is just cool, messy, gross, and fun. You probably want to make it outside.

What You Need:

About ½ cup white glue, a bowl, about ½ cup liquid starch *(you can find this stuff in the laundry section of the grocery store)*, a spoon, green food coloring

What You Do:

1. Pour the glue into the bowl.
2. Add the liquid starch.
3. Add two drops of the green food coloring.
4. Use the spoon to stir like crazy until it's mixed.
5. Let it sit for about five minutes.
6. Use your hands and mix it up until it all comes together.
7. Just when you think you must have done something wrong, it turns into this drippy, stretchy, messy slime.

Disappearing Ink

Technically, this is disappearing
and then reappearing ink.
Perfect for secret messages.

What You Need:
A toothpick, lemon juice (just squeeze a lemon into a dish),
white paper, a lamp with the lightbulb exposed (*don't use a
megawatt bulb, just something that warms up*)

What You Do:
1. Dip the toothpick into the lemon juice and write a secret
   message on the paper.
2. Let it dry—the "ink" will disappear.
3. To read the message, hold the paper a few inches away from
   a warm lightbulb—the message will slowly show up. Spooky!

**MAMA'S LITTLE
SECRET**

▸ ▸ ▸ ▸ ▸ ▸ ▸ ▸

Lemon juice is relatively clear,
so it makes a mark when
it's wet but dries transparent.
It also contains carbon. When
heated, the carbon darkens,
which allows you to read
the message.

Be a Spooky Gypsy Fortune Teller

This is a fun trick to play at a Halloween party.

1. Write fortunes with disappearing ink *(see page 137)* for each of the guests and let them dry completely beforehand.
2. Have each guest select a "blank" piece of paper.
3. One by one, they can come to you to get their fortunes read.
4. Set yourself up at a table with a warm heating pad under a scarf on your lap.
5. Close your eyes and take the paper. Place it on the table.
6. Cover it with the heating pad, covered by your scarf.
7. Hold it under your scarf and hum.
8. Check the paper and when the fortune shows up, act exhausted.

✳ ✳ ✳ ✳ ✳ CLEVER MAMA ✳ ✳ ✳ ✳ ✳

ELEVEN COOL SHARK FACTS

1. A shark's skin is covered in tiny, sharp teeth called denticles. In the past, people commonly used sharkskin as sandpaper!
2. Sharks have been around since way before dinosaurs—about 400 million years—and they haven't changed much over time!
3. Sharks' teeth are normally replaced every eight days.
4. A shark may grow, use, and shed over 20,000 teeth in its lifetime!
5. Two-thirds of a shark's brain is dedicated to its keenest sense—smell.
6. Sharks are such amazing hunters because they have a sensory system called the ampullae of Lorenzini that they use to *feel* the vibrations, heartbeats, and muscle movements coming from their prey.
7. Great white sharks can go as long as three months without eating.
8. More people are killed each year by dogs, pigs, or deer than by sharks.
9. Sharks have no bones. A shark's skeleton is made up of cartilage.
10. The average lifespan of a shark is 25 years, but some sharks can live to be 100.
11. Most sharks need to be in constant movement to stay alive.

Turn a Glass of Water Upside Down Without Spilling a Drop

Can't keep the kids interested in water? Has the tried-and-true thirst quencher lost its pizzazz? Turn things upside down for a real jaw-dropper!

What You Need:
A glass, water, a playing card or an index card *(big enough to cover the opening of the glass)*

What You Do:
1. Fill your glass up to the very top with tap water. The water should come right up to the lip of the glass.
2. With a flourish, cover the glass with the card. Make eye contact, and pause to build suspense.
3. Holding the card in place, turn the glass upside down.

4 Carefully remove your hand, leaving the card in place. *(Don't jiggle the card!)*

5 Hold the water over your head if you dare! The card stays put, and the water stays inside the glass, even though it's upside down!

MAMA'S LITTLE SECRET
▸ ▸ ▸ ▸ ▸ ▸ ▸ ▸

How does the card defy gravity? It's all about atmospheric pressure. The weight of the atmosphere is pushing in on us from all angles at all times. It pushes down on us, pushes in on our sides, and even pushes up. It's everywhere! When you placed the card over the glass, you made the pressure on the outside pushing in the same as that pushing out. When you flipped it over, the pressure of the atmosphere pushing in was a balance, holding the card in place. Bump the card and whoosh! Gravity comes into play and the water comes pouring out.

Blow Up a Balloon with a Bottle

Who knew you could amaze and amuse so much with an empty soda bottle? Well, Mama did.

What You Need:
A balloon, an empty plastic two-liter soda bottle, 1 cup white vinegar, 2 tablespoons baking soda

What You Do:

1. Announce that you will blow up a balloon without ever putting it to your mouth.
2. Show the kids the balloon.
3. Pull out your bottle.
4. Pour the vinegar into the bottle.
5. Take a spoon and put the baking soda into the balloon.
6. Stretch the neck of the balloon over the mouth of the bottle, keeping the head of the balloon draped down to make sure none of the baking soda falls into the bottle yet.
7. When the seal is complete, lift the balloon and let the baking soda fall into the vinegar.
8. Watch the reaction and let go—the balloon will inflate.
9. You can add drama by holding the mouth of the bottle and acting as if it might explode.
10. If you're lucky, it may explode!
11. When the kids settle down, you can pry the balloon off the bottle and get a great raspberry sound.

Magic Finger Optical Illusion

This simple optical illusion is a great distraction, and all you need is fingers and a blank wall.

What You Do:

1. Have the kids look at a blank wall. It should be at least six feet away.
2. Then they should hold their arms out in front of them and bend their wrists, so their two index fingers are pointing at each other. Tell them to keep focused on the wall and bring their fingers together.
3. A floating finger should appear between their two index fingers.

Pierce a Balloon with a Needle without Popping It

I confess to using this trick to show how gentle I am with a needle when my boys get splinters. It's simply amazing, and it assures them of my needle-wielding talents.

What You Need:
A balloon, a small piece of tape, a needle

What You Do:
1. Blow up your balloon.
2. Ask the kids to inspect it.
3. Conceal a stamp-size piece of tape on the index finger of your left hand. When the balloon is passed back to you, discreetly place the tape on the balloon, near the neck.
4. Hold the needle up. Pause for effect.
5. Place the needle into the center of the tape. Squint, as if you expect the worst.
6. Push the needle in as far as it will go.
7. Remove the needle.
8. Look smug.

MAMA'S LITTLE SECRET
▸ ▸ ▸ ▸ ▸ ▸ ▸ ▸

Usually when you poke a needle into a balloon, it explodes because the air in the balloon rushes to leave out of that opening all at once destroying the balloon in the process. The tape provides strength to the wall of the balloon and protects it from getting destroyed.

Morse Code

Spend an evening teaching this code to the kids and you can use it in the dark with flashlights, tapping glasses across the room, or even exchanging secret notes. There should be a short pause between letters, and a longer one between words.

A ·—	O ———	2 ··———
B —···	P ·——·	3 ···——
C —·—·	Q ——·—	4 ····—
D —··	R ·—·	5 ·····
E ·	S ···	6 —····
F ··—·	T —	7 ——···
G ——·	U ··—	8 ———··
H ····	V ···—	9 ————·
I ··	W ·——	period
J ·———	X —··—	·—·—·—
K —·—	Y —·——	comma
L ·—··	Z ——··	——··——
M ——	0 —————	question mark
N —··	1 ·————	··——··

Eak-spay Ig-pay Atin-lay! (Speak Pig Latin)

What's cooler than a mama who can speak different languages? This is easy. All you do is take the first sound of a word and add an "–ay" sound, and then stick it at the end of the word. Confused? Look:

Take the word *zebra*, for example. In pig Latin, it's now *ebra-zay*. Here are some more:

Book=Ook-bay
Cat=At-cay
Dog=Og-day

Get it? For words that begin with a vowel, just add -yay to the end of the word:

Apple-yay
Elephant-yay

Ave-hay un-fay!